CO   LONGER POEMS

HAYDEN CARRUTH

COLLECTED LONGER POEMS

COPPER CANYON PRESS

Acknowledgments: "Asylum" was originally published in *The Crow and
the Heart* (Macmillan) thanks to Emile Capouya. *Journey to a Known Place*
was originally published in a limited edition by New Directions, many thanks
to James Laughlin. *North Winter* was published by Prairie Press thanks to
Carroll Coleman. *Contra Mortem* was published as a chapbook by the Crows Mark
Press. These poems and "My Father's Face" were republished in *For You*;
thanks for permission to reprint to James Laughlin and New Directions.
"Michigan Water" was originally published in *Nothing for Tigers* (Macmillan).
The Mythology of Dark and Light and *Mother* were published as chapbooks by Tamarack
Press, thanks to Allen Hoey, and *Mother* was later included in *Tell Me Again How
the White Heron Rises and Flies Across the Nacreous River at Twilight Toward the Distant Islands*;
thanks to James Laughlin and New Directions for permission to reprint. "Vermont"
was published in *Brothers, I Loved You All* (Sheep Meadow Press), thanks to Stanley
& Moss. *The Sleeping Beauty* was published as a separate volume by Harper & Row;
many thanks to Ted Solotaroff for all his help and attention. It was later republished in
a revised edition by Copper Canyon Press, many thanks to Sam Hamill, to whom also,
and to Tree Swenson, my most profound gratitude for this present volume.

Publication of this book is supported by a grant from
the National Endowment for the Arts and a grant from the Lannan Foundation.
Additional support to Copper Canyon Press has been provided by the
Andrew W. Mellon Foundation, the Lila Wallace–Reader's Digest Fund, and the
Washington State Arts Commission. Copper Canyon Press is in
residence with Centrum at Fort Worden State Park.

Library of Congress Cataloging-in-Publication Data
Carruth, Hayden, 1921–
[Poems. Selections]
Collected longer poems / Hayden Carruth.
p. cm.
ISBN 1-55659-058-X – ISBN 1-55659-059-8
I. Title.
PS3505.A77594A6 1993
811'.54 – dc20 93-11404

COPPER CANYON PRESS
P.O. Box 271, Port Townsend, Washington 98368

This book is for
JOE-ANNE McLAUGHLIN CARRUTH

NOTE

Here in this book are the longer poems I wish to keep in print. Some people will say I am mistaken, e.g., that "The Asylum" is a stiff early unsuccessful work and ought to be omitted, or that "Vermont" is so close in substance to many pieces in the *Collected Shorter Poems* that it should have been included there. Well, I have my reasons. "The Asylum" isn't as good as I wish, but it deals with aspects of my experience in the psychiatric hospital which are not dealt with elsewhere, and moreover it introduces the form I invented at that time called the "paragraph," which reappears, prosodically loosened, in "Contra Mortem" and again, loosened further, in "The Sleeping Beauty." (Critics have called my paragraph a sonnet sometimes, but sonnet-writers will see the difference. The paragraph has its own qualities and problems.) As for "Vermont," it *is* a long poem and the *Collected Shorter* was already overburdened. In fact all the poems here are rather long – though only "The Sleeping Beauty" was written with "epical" intent – and of course this is the main reason for offering them separately.

When people ask which is my favorite among all the poems I've written I sometimes say "Contra Mortem" because it really does what I wanted it to do and perhaps also because it hasn't made much impression on other people – forgive my perversity. But actually many are favorites, and for many reasons. These two collected volumes do contain all the poems of mine that are variously important to me, except a few eliminated from the *Collected Shorter* for lack of space and a few more written since the last poem in that book.

What shall I say to my readers finally after fifty years of writing? It's difficult. To me the passion in these works is plain and compelling, but how unreliable a thing that is! Beyond passion, I think, lie primarily honesty, charity, and a radical attitude, which have also been my guides. I hope these will be plain and compelling to all.

H. C.

17 December 1992

TABLE OF CONTENTS*

The dates after titles indicate times of composition, not publication.

COLLECTED
LONGER POEMS

THE ASYLUM

I came to this place one November day.
Mauve walls rose up then tranquilly, and still
Must rise to wind-burned eyes that way –
Old brickwork on a hill,
Surfaces of impunity beneath a gray
And listed sky. Yet I could read dismay
There rightward in a twisted beech
Whose nineteen leaves were glittering, each
A tear in a rigid eye caught in the pale
Deep-pouring wind. Now these walls
Are thin against the dense insistent gale,
No good when the wind talks in our halls,
Useless at night when these high window bars
Catch every whisper of wind that comes and falls,
Speaking, across my catacomb of stars.

2

Winds; words of the wind; rumor of great walls pierced
Like these, windward, but bomb-pierced. I know. Sun
Burnished the gape, spilled through, dispersed
In lumps of fume. Someone
Removed his helmet. Sorrow-stunned at first
We stood, even we, dunced at such grave bomb-burst,
But then groped forward through the nave.
Wind in a ruined choir. None save
A pigeon to meet us, bird fabulously white
That rose as we came near,
Fluttering and climbing the cascade of sunlight,
Quick wing-clamor in cumbrous air,
And vanished, left us there in that wrecked church.
Silence then; only the old world's wind to hear.
But we, with rifles poised, kept on our search.

3

Wind is a stealth of memory. Footsteps fall,
Dry leaves rustling, a woman of the proud South

Pacing her darkened entrance hall,
Once met there mouth to mouth,
A marvel in love and gravely beautiful,
O dreaming wind! Yet, dearest, I recall
Nine cities where your absolute art
Was love, making the meaning part
Of all madness, myth and history, hard earth
And its hard cities. This endures,
Bodiless in your skill; no violence or dearth
Can harm it, nor mortality that stirs
Like sounds in the wall. You are gone? This power,
So classical, is here and now and yours.
Wrack of the wind, dream-wrack, and then this flower.

4

I hurt. Hungrier flowers try my rank ground.
Indelible, one drifts across Japan,
Rooted as if its stem were wound
Into the heart of a man.
A crumpling sky, a blurted dawn – the sound
Of history burst the years and history drowned.
We lived. An aftersilence fell
Like a wave flooding the plains of hell,
For what word matters? Pity? Shame? The roots
Try my breast-cage, my bone
Gleams in the rot. I hear you, sir, cahoots
Calling from many a dolmen stone,
Murther, murther! Come on then, jacket me,
A flawed mind's falling. Look, the petals bloom
On an idle wind, far, far out to sea!

5

But once winds lightened, freshening fair from the West.
Hayscent, grandfather told me, filled the plain.
Then came the Great Man, voice possessed,
Broad brow and flashing mane,
Chanting the silver words of labor blest,

Deliverance come for God's folk all oppressed.
And the city at the prairie edge
Rises to meet him. Poets pledge
His name to glory, sweet locust blooms in the park.
"Onward!" And triumph fills
Men's eyes. (Not who, but that he came.) The dark
Is fading. See, the sunlight spills
Like silver down the street. Onward! How slow
The years have been. And onward! Freedom wills
The day. (But this all happened long ago.)

6

It was our city too. Chrome and glass
Pitched in the splintering sun, a clumsy wind
Poking the avenue's crevasse,
Lifting old papers. Rescind
Such desultory years before we pass!
Something like that we pled, and spoke of class,
Betrayal, alienation. But . . .
Then as the doors that had been shut
Opened, and we could see within, and saw
Nothing, one by one,
And felt at our backs the wind like a dead claw
And in our brains the splinters of sun,
We tried to hurry, breathless, stumbling, tried
To find a way. But everything was done.
Belching, grinning, all the doors swung wide.

7

What does this wind say, plunging upon the land,
Torrents sinuous and thick? Shall
A long wind make me understand
One separable from all?
Ethics is not a study I had planned.
At the beginning is one cruel command:
Save thou thyself. But where? Dear crowd,
My dear little mad folk, cry loud,

Cry long, add your beseeching to this wind!
For it is a curious blast,
Both full and faint, as if my ears were dinned
By pulses not my own, but past.
Dusk, and the Troy fires wink below our hill.
And here we came to search the self at last,
And here the long wind comes, and comes to kill.

8

Gnarled wind blurs the light, my hurt and another's.
Yet his the more for that he knew twilight
At Hautefort, taught there by his guild-brothers,
En Arnaut for one, whose sight
Was music. And what has come of it? Wind smothers
And snuffs our looking. And he sought also the others
Deep in the tongues, makers who wrought
The clear eye-path newly. And what
Has come of it? And he gave us instruction, he that made
His canzos truly, he
That discovered again the shift and poise that weighed
In our speaking, heron wing and the sea.
And what has come of it? For he of us all had risen
To history, taking wide compass, curiously,
Now all hideous, false and false, rotting in wind's prison.

9

But if the wind should fall and silence spread
Like nightward dimness rising underseas,
Muffling many a fervid head,
Stilling the quick-tongued trees,
Stagnation creeping, loathed, in board and bed,
The weed, the bone, the dust, the spider's thread,
If nerve-song were suppressed to quell
Our quick wise hurting, if a smell
Of sleep-rot issued from us, black slime boiled
From our close scaly wall,
Water clotted and air's befoulment coiled

On each lost creature that could crawl
Apart beneath the mountainous dung-soft sky,
If this should be and if the wind should fall,
Could sane men live? Dear friends, could madmen die?

10

I came to this place one November day.
The winter deepened. Then at last came March,
Then May, and now another May,
Our outdoor season. A larch,
Of graceful habit, mounts its green display,
And we have almost nothing left to say.
Motley despondent pigeons pass
Like tick and tock across the grass.
The nurse assigned to govern shuffleboard
Is continually amazed,
Being young and pretty. The male attendants hoard
Their tedium like whiskey, poised
For anything. Up where the roofs are pearled
By sunlight, an arrow turns forever, seized
In our four winds, pointing across the world.

11

This nation was asylum when we came
On sea-qualms heaving west in wind-drenched ships
And found our plenty. But the home
We built here in these strips
Of wilderness could not resist the storm
That trailed us. It foundered like a tomb
Whose broken walls cannot protect
The dead from the toothy wind of fact.
Always this breaking. And is not the whole earth
Asylum? Is mankind
In refuge? Here is where we fled in birth.
Yet what we fled from we shall find,
It fills us now. And we shall search the air,

Turning drained eyes along the wind, as blind
Men do, but never find asylum here.

12

Then ultimately asylum is the soul.
Reason curls like a nut in wrinkled sleep,
And here, here on this windy knoll,
Our house was built to keep
One private semblance where we conceive our role.
Thus when our solemn inspectors come to stroll
The shadeless halls, our wives and friends,
We seldom mention how the winds
Shriek in their mouths. Gradually we feel
More natural, we try
To sink like the silent leaves that slide and reel
In anguish down the windy sky.
Sometimes it works. Sometimes we find out then
Our tiny irreducible selves. We die.
And after that we die again, again.

13

Persimmon wind, lost names raining. Thwart
Of forgetfulness! Lady, I'm a breath,
A puff in bare bones, a dry heart,
A small particular death,
And here I am – this death, the unquestionable part
Of reason. Good night. The bones assert
What the bones know, and love will follow,
Follow. My sweetheart, fellow,
I lived with you, but now with these, all gone
Stark crazy. If love fails
To soothe such pain and runs like the salt sea down
The wounds of these particular halls,
Good night. Good-bye. Here's darkness and rain
And a small wind in broken walls, dear walls.
Here am I – drowned, living, loving, and insane.

JOURNEY TO
A KNOWN PLACE

1. TERRA

Tundra, the distant marches. And wind veering, clatter of steely grasses;
Steady tramontane pummeling eye and bone.
Between hummocks the ice-shell, glinting,
Splintered under our tread, slashing our shoes,
        the papery leather
        flaking, crumbling.
And the earth reached before us and behind us
And at our sides to the imperceivable horizon,
And direction wavered and slued in the barrenness.
Yet we followed without question, led without hesitation,
Our line, ophidian, dividing the wilderness,
        the left hand
        and the right hand.
We were the journeyers, we were the vexed and doubtful folk.
And this was the journey to the ships, and we knew only,
Marching in disorder,
Driven or staggered by dry frozen wind,
That at the end of our endless file,
On a day among many, indistinguishable,
Would lie the two ships of our destination,
        the ship of the red sail,
        the ship of the white sail,
And which vessel to choose was a matter of contention among us.
I heard the tanglement of voices, demanding, cajoling,
"The red sail!" "The white sail!" "The red . . ."
And the wind veered, bending the steely grasses.
At night the moon shed a shadowless whiteness,
And I wondered if this were the true color of lunacy,
Or if the slow fiery sun, glowing without warmth,
Resembled the day of our ultimate despair.
We spoke in the voice of our fathers,
Utterance laden with prophecy, clerical and severe.
Occasionally as we advanced into the vastness before us
Machines of the recent wars appeared by the way,
Shattered and desolate,
Akimbo,
Swart with the gangrenous rust.

And the ginger snake made haste on the frozen land.
We encountered too the camps of the untidy aged,
> a few sticks and a
> tentcloth flapping;
Madwomen of exhaustion, loose-eyed, the leer of defeat,
The patriarch's paw-handed shame.
And still the column moved in continual clamor,
> the voices shouting,
> crying and contending,
And some were there who walked backwards in the heat of the argument,
Gesturing in antagonism.
And in the confusion of voices I sickened, but went onward.
Once in the hard light a blade shone, and the victim lay writhing.
I cried out, shortly, as in the voice of a woman, and passed on with the rest.
In the closeness of people was no warmth, for the wind flowed among us,
But a surge and stink of bodies like the huge discord of voices.
Vomit cringed in my throat.
And after a time, how long I do not remember,
Earth in its flatness ended in the flat sea
Where the two ships lay at their wharves,
> others attending offshore.
And the sky reeled in hysteria, gulls screaming for a bit of meat;
Nor did our tumult diminish,
But men fought, often with women and children, cursing and struggling,
Often with one another in explosions of fury,
Claiming here historical necessity, claiming there the divine will,
> and we had no unreadiness
> of combative slogans.
And men dragged one another aboard the ships,
Others filling the beaches with confusion,
The absolutists cauled in the beast of fear;
For this was the mammoth conglomerate,
The throbbed gland and the wormy nerve, the voice-box quaking.
And when in our midst the two ships moved from their moorings,
Crowded with men and women and their children in multitude,
Some were pushed over the sides and into the sea,
> and others leapt willingly.
In the gray sloping waters heads bobbed like rotten fruit,
And there came two more ships immediately.

I too was thrown this way and that in the throng
And shaken in my sickness like a leaf on a great tree
      with the autumn wind blowing,
And I drifted apart, stumbling and fitful,
And eddied away, swinging on windy voices, the terrible land behind me,
And so entered the sea.

II. AQUA

Colder than land is the random sea, shriveling
    Vein and sinew as the long tow took me, tumbled me,
        Forward and down through the waves wheeling and plunging,

Ram-herds curled in their charge to the restless demon,
    The bugling weather; and I forward and down in the chambers
        Of amethystine light. Outward the deeper sluices, swaying,

Rocked me in the sea's exhaustless movements, heaving
    In tidal energy, while coldness seeped almost sweetly
        Into my heart and a numbness as of some grave and true

Dispassion altered my thoughts. Such was awareness
    Of solitude, the calla silence abloom in decaying voices,
        The ripe rot of the years. For alone I moved where serpentine

Sea-plants with flexive gestures swung in the waters,
    Dancing the laziest sarabande in the primary darkness,
        And downward the dimness of interiors opened before me.

Wavering fishes, the febrile schools, silver and gold,
    Shone gloomily beyond my fingertips, which extended
        Will-lessly in the waters, bending in the cadences of a

Dream. And the lobster flounced on the sand, mad
    Claws dragging a wasp's body; the grampus plied there
        In the unctuous waters, and the blowfish stuffed with fear;

I saw the manatee browsing, imperturbable, obese;
    The halibut, twisted and anguish-eyed, fled from himself;

Ten thousand herring marched right oblique at unison's mute

Command. Down, down to the stiller mid-regions
   Where giant sea-snails hung torpid in copulation
      Half out of their shells, white flesh rolling, exposed

Obscenely in the slow coiling and cramping of a cruel
   And monstrously deliberate ecstasy. And I looked away
      In my boredom, but other snails hung also before my eyes

Everywhere, coupling identically, an abhorrent multitude;
   Until they also rose at last above me. The far sea-floor
      Appeared in the gloom, black pinnacles mounting. I saw the

Black roving shark, voracity finned and aprowl, impatient,
   Powerful, rip-toothed for the living prey, there and now
      Here, hunting, hunting; and the shapes of lost fantasies,

Every carnality, slithered and lurked on the primitive rock.
   Massive eels upheaved and subsided. Blind mouths, vulviform,
      Maneuvered in the lewd ingestive suck. Brilliant anemones

Took down their prey convulsively from the waters.
   Still I moved downward, drifting unharmed in the carnage,
      Down to the bottommost cave which I knew would contain

The great beast of the sea, primal, supreme. And the
   Ultimate cold of the depths lapsed softly into my flesh,
      Obscurely, like a casual cry in the night. And I came then

To the cave where the monster awaited me, many-armed
   And dark, a slow aimless uncoiling of tentacles; and
      Passively, for I knew no force of movement, I floated

Into the entanglement of an embrace that flowed around
   Me like the toils of an immobilizing ether. Coldness
      Consumed my brain. And the great beast's webbed grasp

Drew me close to his enormous baleful eyes, and he peered

Into me, so that I knew him, and from my revulsion, deep
    And beyond fear, the salt of my eyes was borne to join the

Sea's. I slept, and awoke on a shore where the air was
    Bright; and above me, extending to the height at which
       Vision dissolves in aspiration, a mountain rose from the sea.

III. AER

Air
    in its brightness
          moist
          and warm
Bore my ascent now,
          eddying and
Upcoursing.
       For I toiled now,
Walked limping
       (injured! so
In the hiding
       might of the sea)
And lurched
       on the rocks. But
Sinuous winds
      urged me,
      aided me,
          flowing,
Curling in supple rills
        over my
Body,
     mounting upward continually.
Sleep-purged,
      awake now,
         thighs and
Back straining,
      nervy;
        and the rich
Wind
     humming with spice,

                              deep-laden.
An eagle
              became my companion,
Riding
              the currents, broad wings
Guiding me
Upward on plume and freshet.
                                        Simoon
Rolled in the gullies,
                              the hot
                              breeze
Heavy with sweet dew,
                                        pungent,
Lifting
              close to my shoulders. And
I leaned
              to my limp,
                              learning,

Swinging
              at last on my wound, up-
Ward,
              long-gaited,
                              and the steeps
Sheering
Above me
              pronounced my eagerness.
Let it be said again. The tunes
Of the harp are in the strings and
The sequences thereof.
                                        Hear these
Inward parts,
              hear them shimmering.
The wholeness grows in itself, so,
Like the western sky
                              ascending at
Sunset,
              intricate, aureate, and free.
And my guide returned,

                        dallying
                                on the wind,
Broad wings
                        as of my spirit now
Shaped
                to the structures
                                of air,
The rilled air
                        curving,
                        flowing;
                                        wings to
Beat
                on the sudden blast,
                                        lone as
I; we two moving,
                                skilled now in the
Profound and lovely
Necessities,
                        mutenesses,
                                the sturdy
                                moments.
Look, look!
                        Pride and courage
(A bird's eyes)
                        but also
                                (more
Fiercely)
                honesty
                                (honor's dint),
The inner appraisal
                                and submission,
Such as is given to animals
                                        (without
Hope of the want of it)
                                granting
Less the seen power to fulfill need
Than the need itself.
                                So much must
One do in loneliness,

              so much shyly
In freedom.
           And in long afternoon
I rested,
        drenched in air. And there
Heard the eagle's voice
             above me
Where he alit
         on a scarped tor,
                and
At first laughter
         bulged on my lips
For what I heard,
         feeble and shrill;
But quickly I understood,
             this was
The eagle's song,
         and in it I heard
How he used his voice well and fully
In the ancient way,
         and I heard also
How the beauty of it
         came in this use,
How the song throve in the wind,
Fared outward among rocks and steeps,
Ventured and returned,
         became,
             was
Eloquence of the mountain
         (that
Shrillness, tone of flint),
         singing
The whole selfhood of loftiness
And of rock
        and of the liquorish air
And of all the names of that good place.
And in listening
        my ears forgot
The woolly sweat clinging, ear-moss,

And I heard in the song,
                              that voice
Raised to the genius of mount and rock,
My being,
                    sentient and known. Onward
We went then until
                              toward nightfall
Hunger overcame me,
                                        and the bird
                                        saw my distress
And brought me an egg which was,
                                                      I
Knew,
            a work made in the manner of
Perfection.
                    And I broke it and
Ate the contents,
                              and that night I
                              slept peacefully
In the ocher moonlight,
                                        dreaming of
Dry heads spiked smiling high on
An old bridge,
                              and in my dream
                                                      the
Heads sang
                    melodiously, all in a tune.
In the morning
                              I rose and resumed
My journey,
                    stepping on the winds,
The great bird
                              ever near me.
                                                Air
Turning,
            soaring;
                              and I – no more
                              the marauder.
When the sun stood

                        near the zenith
The eagle left me,
                        wheeling away in a
Circle
        widely,
                so that my eye
                following him
Saw the sea outstretched, blue and
Blazed with the plumy grain,
                                ocean's
Wide-marching corn;
                        and the ships,
                                        so
Many, putting out from the mountain,
A wind-tossing
                of bright pennants,
Moving;
        and off
                        remotely, on the far
Curve of earth,
                        land yellow and vert,
Ornamented.
                        Yes, Lyonesse, Atlantis,
Gay Wyoming.
                        And when I looked again
To the eagle
                he had risen far above me
                and above the mountain,
High
        on the vortical currents
                                        soaring
Into
        the blinding depths of the sun.

        IV. IGNIS
Upward into the dome of brilliance, limping:
I, the tired climber, acquiring strength
From fatigue, weakness repaired in desire;

I, mounting, going where the stout clumps
Of wild wheat purply ripened, among rocks
Glowing like porcelain now, like jade, among
Silken grasses flowing in flame-like waves,
Among the increasing flowers, thickening trees,
The purslane bedded between the roots of oak,
Aspiring now in sun's cascading element,
Splendors upbranching, the palpitant leafing blood.

Sing, little voice,
Of the sun, lordly
And lovely, eloquent
Boy of the light
So meaning, so dumb
That at last it is
This one, the small one,
Our princeling who levels us,
Marries us, tumbles us,
Scarred or untouched,
In the crowded garden.
Sing, little voice,
The imperfect song
Of done and done,
Imperfect and wrong:
Right with the sun,
Our infant, lordly
And lovely, leveling
All. For the light
Alone does pierce
Armor and shell
And the knurling skull,
Giving done and done,
One and one,
To behold: each
In each. Inward
The light enters
Each darkness alike,
And in similitude
Is understanding.

Sing, little voice,
The imperfect song
Of gratefulness
As my shadow,
Handsomer, sings.

"Light, which moves at the rate of 186,000 miles
Per second, requires 100,000 years to cross
From one rim of our galaxy to the other rim."
Tell me, I murmured, tell me what does it mean
At this way station? For God's sake, interpret
Me this, I mumbled. "The light-sensitive elements
Of the human retina number 1,000 billions . . ."
Nailed to the raft of sense, swept by the magnitudes.

Upward into the dome of brilliance, limping:
And the gemlike rock glowed under the mosses,
And ferns splayed like cool flames, and trees
Lifted, arching and strained to the august sky;
And there were open places where I found
Other journeyers, resting or climbing, strangers,
Sweet eyes once cracked in the torturing cold;
And some few I saw known to me, and one was
A woman I had once married, now like a soft ash
Inly aglow, rippling the violet of mind's smile
Like the concentricities of a woodland pool.
And our hands' touching sang the small cockcrow
As for night's ending, across the distant fields.
So through the alert forests we advanced
Together, by streams that leapt faultlessly
To the far nether sea, crystalline, syllabled,
By savor's herbs, spilt flowers on the way,
The vines and berry trees bright with their meat,
Each blossom in separate need conjointly gendered,
Simple and brave, shaped by a seasonal sap
To the forms of earth in its sovereign histories;
And so we two, there in a private place
Of hot endeavor, as root and bud and bloom,
The bronze sky ringing above, the wild wheat singing.

Proven never,
Being riven
By a steely word
That seals and deafens,
Till, until
One is but one
And all affrighted,
Lone, alone –
Still no treason,
Time or distance,
Quells the quick
Supposing faith;
Will and reason
Drive the breath:
You, you, you.

And I had seen the scarred small breast
Of the hurt woman, imperfect, wounded, wakening
In my body the honeyed and flowing anguish
Of her being weighed on my lameness: but it
Was love. And afterward we went on,
Climbing together into the fire, the flames
Seeming to touch us, flittering on our arms,
Purifying us, so that the shimmer and gleam
Moved between us as the force of our desire,
Altering in our humility beyond desire
To acceptance, each of himself in the other truly;
And of these still other ones, these multitudes
Converging now as the mount narrowed,
Moving upward together in need as food of
The earth, up in the heat of the marrying sun.

Light is the force that alone resists the wind,
Stays, unwavering, though the wind sweeps by.

And often our hands reached out in guidance
Or assistance, for scarcely a one was unwounded
And eyes I saw ill placed in the mask of shock.

Yes, tongues had been torn out, backs
Had been furrowed with lashes, many an eye
Blinded, many a limb broken, and the
Able of body walked with a shackling gait.
In truth this journey was the painfulest,
Gravest; and in this we knew one another,
Losing for a rare time the futility of words.

    To stake it all,
    The need and the response,
    The point from which
    Intelligence went forth,
    The failing quality
    Of aspiration
    In which one found
    One's strength, the walled
    Terrors in which one
    Found love, and finally
    The indifferent space
    Everywhere dividing
    Individual worth,
    To stake it all
    On a flawed, soft,
    Abused and unreliable,
    Imperfect word:
    Magnanimity.

And up, far, far, the astral banks, and then?
Nowhereness broods there? Contemplates this hatch?
Dictum, denial: either way absurd.
And that's the horror, that too in part of the song.

To the last woodland ridge, to the summit we came,
Where the forest parted, withdrew from the broadening road,
And where in the humming sun the journeyers gathered,
Groups walking easily now, the highways converging;
And when with a murmur and extending of arms we came
To the place where the city of gold lay visible,
We paused briefly to marvel, and passed on to the

Avenues continuing among scenes of consummate
Splendor, arches and arabesque all agleam in the
Sun, the golden and emerald tiles, and the folk there,
Both the fair-born ones of the city and those others,
Our immigrant people, greeting us as we moved
On wondering feet onward, still toward the center.
And we came at last to the park where the city opened
Round an emblazoned zone and the light, liquescent
And shimmering, seemed a golden-roseate intensity,
Seemed as a fountain ascending, whose returning flow
Made the sunfire's cascade, swirling and vaporing.
And in the midst was the great wheel rising, turning
In music and light, where the people rode in their
Separateness all together, ascending and equally
Descending in the light, instructed at each place
Of the wheel's endlessness. And there the multitude
Assembled, crowding in the unity of concord, all
Estates and relations of being but chiefly the
Female and the male together, joined in desire's
Known imperfectibilities, the great loves with the less,
Always unequal, able and unable making
Each of his opposite anguish the cause of love,
And this was a real urbanity. Holiday, holiday,
The sun and the wheel, and my companion and I
Hand in hand by the edge of the park; until
We also stepped forward, identities, we with the
Others, the gimp and the aging lady, two notes
Of the flute. And for once unambiguously
All was turned to account; and I saw how the
Bitter bitter shame, terror, quick retaliation
And lust, yes, even ignorance that is called evil,
The enormous relative compassment complete,
The rebellion too, the heart's grand assertions
Against the ruins of broken works and days,
All fact, all dream – how from this we make,
Each in his only ascertainable center,
The world of realization, the suffered reality,
Through which comes understanding; or, if not
Understanding, at least the person fleshed

Sufficiently, sufficiently in love's fragments
That gleam in the rubbish of cruelty and wrong:
To know what it is to receive what one has given,
As in a kiss, to bear and to be born,
To see the earth beneath the heron's eye.

    Anything ends
    In its beginning,
    The circles turning
    Slowly, so slowly,
    Quern of the beat
    Of the downrunning heart.
    The sunlight fell like diamonds
    But did not slacken
    Remembrance's forewarning
    Of cold and dark to come,
    The journey retaken
    Without end,
    Without end.

And so purity was compounded of impurity.
My spirit rose, a leaf above the fire.
In poverty of means was the authentic end.
Ah, the rack's song. Who shall turn the wheel?
Who shall give up his bones to be parted?
Our guilt contorts the images of our mercy,
But is not our humility more than we thought,
More than a last refuge of the aggressive mind?
And in our knowing, even unto all unknowing,
We are, we are, spite of a foolish end
Under your ancient brightness, O grave stars!
From this we speak and our speech is love,
    Without witness, simply and for the day.

NORTH WINTER

Coming of winter
is a beech sapling
rising silverly
in a brown field
in bramble in
thicket the raspberry
the rosemallow
all gone to rust
a silver sapling
to which in wind
and the judaskisses
of snow the starved
brown leaves cling
and cling.

2

In spring this mountain was a fish
    with blond scales
in summer it was a crab
    with a green shell
in fall it became a leopard
    with a burnished coat
in winter the mountain is a bird
    with lavender feathers
    and a still heart.

3
Snow
    ice
        bitter wind
the body of love.

4
Where two boots labored yesterday across the
    snowdrifted pasture

today each boothole is an offertory of
    bright seeds
bittersweet yellowbirch hemlock pine thistle
    burning unconsumed.

5

Stronger than destiny is pain
and in the leaf
the marvelous venature is stronger
and in the year
the last morsel of pancake
of the forty-third breakfast
is stronger.

6

Caught in the briary stars
a lunar scrap
                blurred
like paper flickering in a gale
carrying away a scarcely remembered
poem of a summer night.

7

Twenty-two degrees below zero
and only the blade of meadow
like a snowpetal or foil of platinum
to defend the house against the glistening
mountain and the near unwinking
moon.

8

Morning ice on the window
opaque as beaten silver
while the poet
in his ninefootsquare hut stamps

rhythmically breathing out plume
after plume of warmth and the stove
nibbles a few frozen sticks.

9

In the snowy woods of morning
the new deer tracks run
cross and criss and circle among
snowapparelled spruces and gray
maples telling of revels by night
of joy and delight and happiness
beyond any power of consciousness
although the small green pellets
mean a hard diet.

1 0

The tamarack with needles lost
and a thousand curled-up twigs
like dead birdsfeet takes
the snow greedily and in snatches
to cover its misshapen nakedness.

1 1

A winter's tale is told in
   rumors of snow
      sneaping winds
the frazil flux of identities
   tardy recognitions
      the living stones.

1 2

Think not of chaste snow always
nor of crystalline coldness think
of spruce boughs like the swordblade
breasts of negresses and of the bull

mountain humped over the white soft
valley and of stags raging down
the rutting wind and of northern
passion crackling like naked trumpets
in the snow under the blazing aurora.

1 3

The song of the gray
ninepointed buck
contains much contains
many contains all
a whole north for
example the sweet
sharp whistling of
the redpolls caught
overhead in the branches
of the yellow birch
like leaves left over
from autumn and at
night the remote
chiming of stars
caught in the tines
of his quiet exaltation.

1 4

The arctic owl moved across the snowsmooth
meadow to the dark balsam without sound
without wingbeat more quiet than a fish
more effortless than the gliding seed
as if it were a white thought of love
moving moving over the pasture to home.

1 5

Five
jays

discuss
goodandevil
in a
white
birch
like five
blue
fingers
playing
a
guitar.

1 6

Eons gone by the sea
in its huge stress
hissed among these promontories

now stilled
in the frozen whirl and floodtide
of the snow.

1 7

Like a frozen lake the sky in the bitterest
twilight cracks and rays of a black elm
rising a spray of limbs reveal
the longdrowned lurid moon.

1 8

The frozen
brook sprawls
in sunlight
a tree of glass
uprooted.

1 9

Cold hunger tripped her but her years
held her downfallen in this snow hollow
this small death valley where small beaks
and talons will slowly chip her frozen
being though in the snow desert she will
not bleach and her eyes will stay soft
and beautiful a long long time in the
winter light and she will modestly wear
her genteel tatters of old flesh and fur.

2 0

Snow buntings whirling
on a snowy field
cutglass reflections
on a ceiling.

2 1

The spaniel flies with his ears
across the snow carrying a
deer's legbone in his jaws
the bone flops threejointedly
and the little hoof dances
delicately in the snow.

2 2

The window
         the icicle
                the gleaming moon
when the lamplight fails.

2 3

Night is a cauldron
of boiling snow

and the highway
where headlights cringe
seethes with a furious froth
and melts away.

   2 4
This wind this
screaming parrot
this springing
wolf this down
fall this ab
solute extinc
tion this deton
ating godhead
this wind this.

   2 5
Blizzard trampling past has left
the birches bent as in humiliation
the soft scotch pines laid down
as in subjection the beeches snapped
at the top as in a reign of terror
the balsams scarred but upright
as in the dignity of suffering and all
the woods in sorrow as if the world
meant something.

   2 6

Pale dawnlight spooks the mist
and the valley glimmers and
higher behind this mountain
whitely rises a farther peak
in remote majesty a presence
silent and unknown and gone
by noon.

27

Harlequin
is said to assimilate himself to a condition
of animal grace

let him study
the forehoof of the pinto searching for grass
in the snowy pasture.

28

In cold
      the snow
leaps and
         dances

lightly
     over the
earth

       but in thaw the sullen
           fingers of snow heavily
      cling to each stalk and to every
          stone.

29

Tracks of the snowshoe rabbit across the
   snow
are a ridiculous ominous alphabet of
   skulls.

30

The brook has holes in its cover
this morning
where the black water flows

rippling menacing
under the snow

which mounds in untouched purity
except where
threaded prints of the mink
delicately deathly
stop to drink.

    3 1
Snow comes
   bits
of light
flake from the sky
day breaks
   whirling
in early night.

Beginning with the palest and softest lavender
deepening
downward
murex
purpure
arras of
old brocade
kingly
loveliest hues
imaginable
snow blending
the naked
hardwood
maples
beeches
birches
forests called
green in summer
now this
unbelievable
intricacy
shaded
purple
gray
hanging
wavering
trembling
over the
valley
this is the wintering mountain.

3 3

Heavy gloves
or better
          mittens
the north silencing
savoring and saving
that lewdword
finger.

3 4

After the thaw after
the illusion cold comes
again
          returning
changed in aspect
a great body of death
and inertia a corpse
flung down
               a whale
perhaps
          gray and still
and immense crushing
everything
               day
becomes hard and silent
night stiffens heaving
to support the weight
while the woods groan
and the soft snow
turns metallic
barren and brittle
the house creaks
under the burden in
mindless suffering
and its nails burst
out with a sound of

cracking bones
               moon
sets in afternoon
jays huddle say
nothing and
               endure.

     3 5
Sky like fishblood
deprecative lurid thin
evening blush on the mountain
and here
          the foreground
very near
          a sheen
vitrescent snowcrust and
reflected light
                thin
lurid and deprecative
                         fish
blood.

     3 6
Gunmetal snow icecolored sky
granitic meadow sullen noon
stunted yellowed loplimbed pine
flayed birch elm decorated
with empty nests poverty
hunger red fingers retracting
in splayed gloves dead sun
gray hair poverty poverty.

     3 7
Wet fire
it turns out
is better than

no
    fire.

   3 8

Sky yellow sky
wet sky reeky
sky lax some
god's old diaper.

   3 9

When some amazonian indians for whom
all experience had been degrees of heat
were given a hunk of ice to touch they said
it's hot
      the eskimo child that tumbled
on the other hand into the fire did not
say it was cold
            nevertheless
                brazil brazil
thy foolishness is also a kind of beauty.

   4 0

The day the brook went out
was still midwinter locked
in zodiacal fastness yet
rain fell and fell in fact
so much the snow turned green
and the water in the brook
covered the ice like urine
until at one crack
the whole damned thing let go
ice and muddy water trees
stones bits of lumber snow
like a racketing express
through a local stop and then

subsided leaving the banks
dark and dirty raw and torn
with new patterns of rocks
looking unfamiliar what
a purgation it was wild
and beautiful and the result
wasn't bad either all told
for now the brook is rising
again after the long
icebound repression singing
a midwinter rebel song.

4 1
Lover of balsam lover of white pine
o crossbill crossbill
cracking unseen with of all things scissors
seeds seeds
a fidget for ears enpomped in the meadow's
silence silence

a crackling thorn aflame in the meadow's
cold cold.

4 2

                                                       i

                                              n f

                                      o e

Snow's downstrokes climb softly up the c   r.

4 3
Lichen and liverwort
laurel and brome
lightened the gravamen
of old stones
a cellarhole far
in foliate woods

a dry cistern
where sweet water stood
a doorstone to nothing
that summer entwined
softly and now
drowned in the snow.

4 4

Astigmatism breaks
the crescent moon
into two images
set asymmetrically
so that they cross
in the upper third
like two scimitars
flung down at rest
on the sahara.

4 5

In freshfallen snow
marks of pad and paw
and even partridge claw
go delicately and distinct
straight as a string of beads
but marks of a heeled boot
waver shuffle wamble
ruckle the snow define
a most unsteady line

then spell it out once

so

death knowledge being heady
it hath not the beasts' beauty
goeth tricksy and ploddy
and usually too damn wordy

but drunken or topsyturvy
gladhanding tea'd or groovy

it arriveth
it arriveth
o you pretty lady.

46

Lichen is a hardy plant
hardy hardy
       taking
sustenance from the granite ledge
nouriture from the dead elm bole
icy plant hoar plant
          living kin
to rime
     the north plant
         flower
of death poverty and resolution.

47

On Lincoln's birthday the forest
bound in fifty degrees of frost
stirs tentatively with a creaking
here and there in the new strength
of the noticeably higher sun.

48

Four greens
    the poplar trunk
    the lichen on the poplar trunk
    the shadow of the poplar over the snow
    the vanished leaves of the poplar fluttering
all across the sky.

49

Under the hill a winter twilight
darkens to evening colorlessly
without sunset and yet the birches
leaping higher across the way
cry pink cry lavender cry saffron
the instant the darkness freezes them.

50

When conditions of frost and
    moisture are just right
    the air is filled
with thousands and thousands
    of points of light
    like the fireflies come back
only tinier and much more brilliant
    as if the fireflies
    had ghosts
to haunt a february night.

51

Three sixteen seventy-
nine five hundred
ten thousand a million
a milliard
           three
a snowsquall
          aged winter's
tantrum in the sun.

52

Small things
    hardest to believe
redpoll snatching
    drops from an icicle.

53

Layer upon layer
      late winter snow
a dobos torte
      compact crusts and fillings
in a cut snowbank counting
      the rings of all winter's
storms and thaws
      like a tree grown
in one season

      to which level
a boot will sink
      depends
on the resistance and
      tensility
of each stratum

      woe to him
who steps where
      sun blared hotly
in january
      he will go in floundering go in
to his chicken neck
      woe woe.

54

In late winter cold nights
and warm days bring
the untimely harvests
bright pails and smoke
in the sugarbush
and the snow known as
cornsnow on the mountain
whining under the skis like
scratchfeed plunging in the chute.

55

The eye of
            the hut
sheds tears
    musically

from the eye of
    the hut
glass tears fall

the tears of
    the hut
shatter and
                trickle
musically away

the hut musically
    is weeping

from the eye of
    the hut
glass tears fall and
    shatter
musically all day.

56

Where the snow bank leans
    let april waken
                let
dishevelment rise from covert
    crocus and violet rise
Persephone lift hand
    to first light
                narrowing
lashes moist from lethe
    dewpetaled diaphane
let the dogtooth

                        following
            fasten in bractlet jaws
sop of the yellow blossom
            and let
                        grasses rise there
unbinding anemone
            arbutus and lethargy
and the dark sward of dreams
            where the snowbank leans.

            5 7
One day music
                        begins
everywhere in the woods
unexpectedly
                        water water
dripping from fir boughs
spilling from ledges
singing
            unexpectedly
as when a woman sleeping
speaks a strange word
or a name
                        so winterfolk
the chickadees give over
harshness for a kind of
carol
            and the poet appears
emerges brushing the
mist from his shoulders
amused and yawning
tasting the snowwater
crumbling a bit of tanbark
in his teeth
                        water water
the pools and freshets
wakening
                        earth glistening

             releasing the ways of
                           the
         words of
                  earth long frozen.

            AFTERWORD:
         WHAT THE POET HAD WRITTEN
. . . and sun the blear sun straggled forever
    on the horizon an unvarying scrutiny around
around as they limped and stumbled holding
    each other against the wind over the ice
that crumbled under them in the tremors of
    unseen currents and the compass plunging
and rearing the sun the livid sun smeared
    in the wind watching watching never
relenting till exhaustion inundated them
    yet they slept with their eyes open clinging
together just as they walked often with
    their eyes shut hand in hand and fell
at last tripped on their destination
    their sextant snagged their compass wild
with incomprehension and they looked
    over the sides of the world   The sun
the bloated sun ever on the horizon ballooning
    and they shuddered and turned to each other
and then dropped down their plumbline
    under them and payed out its knots
hand over hand to the end to fifteen hundred
    fathoms and felt the plummet still swinging in
the void . . .

            . . . nothing they were nothing
    afloat on nothing frozen by the winds of
nothing under the meaningless glare of nothing's
    eye there where the compass points down
there where the needle turns in . . .

　　　　　　　　　　　. . . why
　　had they come so far what had led them
drawn them into the remoteness and the
　　hostility of north what did north mean
and why why was one of them black and
　　the other white these were the points in
doubt　There in confrontation they gave over
　　the last dissemblings and the last nostalgias
nothing against nothing yet more than that
　　their infinitesimal nothing against the
nothing of all the nothing of the real and in
　　this giddiness they became at last
the objectivists　They drew back not in
　　fear for fear had consumed itself
but as the painter retreats from his canvas
　　and so they saved themselves now seeing
how this was the only virtue the withdrawing
　　mind that steadies before reality and they
turned slowly together through the whole
　　arc of absurdity with outstretched hands
bestowing cold benediction on the north
　　and then·sank down　Another confrontation
murdered them as they peered in each other's
　　eyes . . .

　　　　　　　　. . . and saw nothing nothing　Oh
in the low guttural inner voice they proclaimed
　　the misery and destitution of nothing . . .

. . . and saw nothing except yes this is the
　　object nothing except the other's returning
gaze which each knew also saw

　　　　　　　　　　nothing

　　　　　　　　　　　And
　　in this likeness this scrap of likeness that
contained their likelihood they arose once

more calmly the tall twin centers
of compassion in the wide field of cold and
　　horror　And the sun the huge sun circled
around them . . .

　　　　　　　　　. . . they came back trudging
　　in love and hardship while the sun
took a month to set cowering lidless on the
　　extremity of the ice floe where they
crouched　Aurora flickered and mounted
　　pale brightening caparisons of yellow
and green falling fluttering swaying
　　in such majestic movements that that
elemental silence pealed with trumpets
　　and they truly listened with their eyes　Did
they then see with their ears the changing
　　counterpoints of wind and snow the
purity of whiteness modulating everywhere
　　in dunes and fastnesses and cascades
Reality gladdened them and all the more
　　when the astonished walrus fell off his seat
backwards whopping the sea and they smote
　　their knees and wallowed in the snow . . .

. . . north is a horror from which a horror grows
　　a purity and fervor to which in opposition
an equal purity and fervor supervene north
　　is the latitude of the near remote lying
beyond hope and beyond despair lying in destination
　　where the compass points down the needle turns in
where the last breath of meaning is borne away
　　on the cold wind north is the meaninglessness
of beauty uncaused in the complete object
　　auroral flickerings on the eternal snows
the eye swimming in the mind's deluge
　　the blue mountain floating on emptiness
the shadow of the white bear gliding underfoot
　　north is the vacancy that flowers in a

glance wakening compassion and mercy and
    lovingkindness the beautiful dew
of the sea rosmarine the call crying in silence
    so distant so small and meeting
itself in its own silence forever north is
    north is the aurora north is
deliverance emancipation . . .

                    . . . north is
nothing . . .

CONTRA MORTEM

Thirty spokes unite in one nave,
and because of the part where nothing is
we have the use of a wheel.
— Lao-tse

THE BEING

Wherever shadow falls wherever the drowning
of darkness in great light takes waking under
and still awake and still alldiscerning
reaching as if to enter
in anysoever passages or subsurfaces burning
like a dry film upon the inner attaining
of earth of leaf of water of stone
of blood   There murmuring in the din
of a talontaken grievance   There in a flood
seething or in the rattle
of dry snowseas   There trembling for the mood
of hysterical winds deceitful thistles
meteors blooming   There in the huge fire
that rusts every thing away the opening middle
where the world falls in forever   There   There.

THE WOMAN

Among birches moving their white halfnakedness
she dances   And the veils of her being obscure her
or half obscure her for they are her dress
or her undress while nearer
or farther she dances moving effortless
and selfabsorbed like the birches with their sense
of naturalness and when she appears
naked at last having cast to the breeze
her semblances as in her dreams the birches
step intricately before her
or drench her in cooling shadows all the riches
of this presence flowing upon her and through her
making her an object in the true world unknowable
her dance the dance of things without past or future
given and perfect and beyond and inconsolable.

THE CHILD

Otherwise considered being is a force

more or less welldirected   Cometh the child
exploded running nine ways at once
an egg dropped a cup spilled
a universe erupting hell on wheels whence
backward rocking he incautiously squints
in the village square of the square village
to the spire up up and up verge
upon verge higher and higher till he sits
in his damp britches plop
extended a being from his arse to his three wits
real to ideal and then gets up
weeping his laughter dancing his stumble worlding
every unworld eating names in his soup
lowest of low quickest unlife the immense lordling.

The Trees

Birches birches birches true and white
demure of habit and standing on ceremony
bending there left or right
a grove a classical harmony
and yet some secret moves among them   Light
quivers   Is it the aspens twinkling   The night
comes up reining a dark breeze
ruffling the spirit and the near trees
quicken sparkle vanish to the forest
among dogwood and elm
spruce and balsam viburnum and sweet locust
beech rockmaple tamarack alder
a congress a quiet congress for not one leaf intrudes
predominantly   Yet this repose this calm
this being fills the night of the living woods.

The Brook

A threefold obstacle   The center rock
so enormous only a glacial hand could lift it
or settle it in this bed   The hemlock
fallen long since and drifted

into the wide right cleft between rock and bank
stripped by the current denuded of limbs and bark
and yet still green emerald green
with moss and its great crest newgrown
among cardinal flowers   Then in the narrower channel
on the left an iron pot
out at the bottom and at last forever full
The stone the flower the artifact
to mark the brookfall singing flutes in the trees
music never faltering always exact
rising falling in the remote black seas.

THE MOUNTAIN FASTNESS

Beyond and farther and yet from every vantage
rising eternally near crag above crag
this is the upthrust   A tossed village
lies like a trampled flag
at its feet and up there look the ridge
sloughs off the stunted firs like the very selvedge
of earth itself raveled and frayed
where the ground peels back   Call it the void
pulled inside out or the universal grain
in a mindless exultation
sprung from the notgrain   Its climbers learn
footholds too far apart and their own impatience
and death in the dark drops   Call it a comprising
call it the center and edge of every relation
the journeyer's pivot and the journeyer's horizon.

THE VILLAGE

Twilight drivels down the mountain   There below
in slowly gathering shadow the lights come on
lighted windows vague and yellow
and very old   The town
is flecked with light except in the deep hollow
where the graves sink down   Hallowed white and narrow
the steeple rises under a copper fish

swimming in final roselight   The dutch
elm beetle carries his little burden from tree
to tree   Somewhere a dog
barks petulantly across a steel guitar
Ah it is all extraordinarily nostalgic
as people find who come from the city

to fret beneath the police magistrate's famous hatrack
that was the last caribou and now is a pity.

The Fall

Still after the clapper cracked the bell
after the suffocating complicity of the riot
summer's strangling tangling toil
still there came quiet
the colors of mediation in the fall
twilight and robins chirping still and all
potatoes and butternuts laid by
the old bees dreaming how to die
in a drunken reverie by the dripping press
and asters and goldenrod
murmuring darklights through the sleepiness
of completed things   After the blade
had driven through the eye and spilled the gold
something was won some recompense was had
in the histories of anguish quietly told.

The Great Death

Oh if a thousand old folk looked askance
when a puff of cyanide like a colorless wind
seized their gentle world
                          so and
                                    so
                                          who else
observed it   Yet behind
the customary daylight the small dance
of twinkling leaves had darkened and the scenes

that were revisited and tales retold
were not the same   Strangely the world
looked empty and strangely distant as if the stones
themselves had grown absentminded
and had forfeited their presence yet the suns
rose the moons set and people were openhanded
or closefisted as before   The children went back
to school where a few of them comprehended
that what was called their questing was their lack.

THE LITTLE DEATH

Falling plummeting unexpectedly sickeningly
through the region of gray cloud inhabited
by floating objects such as an eye
that grows on a stem a bed
hopping like a rabbit a glass finger a tray
of rings and minnows an artificial boy
a pistol   Descending through this
in rolling qualming swoops helpless
filled with nausea until far far down
far in a distant night
the clouds open on a dark pool and then
a reflected star   With a desolate
cry falling falling falling into the star
the candleflame the spark and through and out
in the noplace where all the nothings never are.

THE COMING OF SNOW

Along the denuded aisles a shadow walks
casting no body bending no branch nor cracking
one dry twig   It sighs and talks
or maybe only the bracken
is mumbling in the wind nothing or no one takes
the time to care   The snow comes a few flakes
unobserved then thicker softening
the raw air almost as in the spring
apple petals falling diffuse the sun

but cold and with a tang
of reality   And though at first they seem to run
him through and vanish on his tongue
slowly he takes an outline and footprints show
the passage he has truly made among
the rubble graces brightening in the snow.

THE MOON

Reflected light reflected again on snow
but beauty is lonely lonely   The snowsurface
is hard gleaming vitrescent blue
without crest or crevice
extending beyond anywhere for long ago
the horizon crumbled in an indeterminate glow
and the night has stillness   Light
that is fragile paleolithic white
from this fossilshell embedded in a sky of shale
conveys a snowgleaming
track for the solitary on and on a trail
of his sole desperation climbing
the world of pure beauty   Remote and high
a real light shimmers an upland farmstead shining
or only a star in the unhorizoned sky.

THE BOOK

Pure beauty is pure being and pure being
is freedom in its most desperate purity
Winter was taintless pythagorean
and meaningless   Then why
was freedom in its purity so unfreeing
why was the world and its lovely snow a thing
so merely coercive like a page
white and unrealized why must rage
in responsibility choose the which and when
and where for each impress
of something particular some character   The pen
wrote freedom's elegy nothing less

than ultimate aggrievement for the cost
of mind's disablement in loneliness
and for the natural things so wrongly lost.

THE THAW

Rigidity nonlife the meaning neither of life
nor of unlife neither a presence nor an absence
but the snowworld the compacted snow and ice
so powerful that the granite
formed in the nuclear sun clicks like the dice
in a crapshooter's hand and shatters a white
incumbency white being the color
of hardness as in the unusual power
of iridium a lithic ideal gripping the forest
in petrifaction bringing
the encompassing the silence the sidereal frost
not just an antisound but a singing
of nothing a reciting of nevertobeborn until
whether near or remote auspicious or menacing
the water by drop by drop by drop begins to fall.

THE STONE

Difficult to think of a stone's gratitude
difficult for that matter to think of stone
essences so various   The white shade
cast by the winter moon
withdraws into covert places and the multiflood
of earthlight often darkly or in tones subdued
by interspersion slowly drenches
the forest the brook the stone   Birches
step forward and the stone rises like an earthspirit
snow dripping from its flanks
burnished and new but scarcely changed a merit
of the abiding between the banks
marking the upstream from down   Its warmth is taken
from another source yet such warmthtaking links
the primal act with this   So the woods waken.

THE WATER

The brook had been frozen almost everywhere   Mounds
of snow had covered the ice serene
and cool as corpseflesh while quiet small sounds
came from the holes where the skein
of black water continued winding   But now
only the scraps and tatters of the snow
are left on the banks and the water
seems purged of darkness brighter
than its winding immanence   In the shallows
where pebbles excite the current
the brook is shaken like the quivering lightandshadow
of aspenleaves or like the cadence
of hundreds of migrant wings flashing in sunlight
against the flow forever far from their nests
and singing singing so pleasantly in their flight.

THE LEAVES

If the sky were green instead of blue its green
would be the aspenleaves which have the same
inlighted sweet intensity of tone
and are the first to come
in spring closefollowed by hickory ash hawthorn
and the rest with butternut last   Each has its own
conception of green some yellow some blue
some like the rockmaple reddish nor
is any leaf precisely like any other
Their tide assaults the mountain
by way of the gradual foothills   Greening breakers
lunge and snap at the heights counting
the evenings forest by forest until the waves
splash on the far high summit announcing
the actual world in the heyday of the leaves.

THE PRIMAVERA

Through the forest across the fair hills away
to compagnas glistening to deltas sparkling

in the suns of finer canticles to the bois
to the luckenwalde to arden
to the name of every woods sung in a heartcry
see the dog run   Light as a wish free
as a thought he runs with his nose to the ground
raising his bellvoice gone and returned
on his keen inquisitive course as swift as an echo
and the prints of his paws are flowers
and the shaking of his coat is the soft rain and the glow
of his eyes is the making of nests his terror
is the scourging of somnolence for he is the dog of spring
and in his going and his returning lie the powers
of extension and concretion that make and remake all being.

THE WOMAN'S GENITALS

Oh this world and oh this dear worldbody
see how it has become become become
how it has flowered and how it has put on gaudy
appearances how it is a plum
in its ripening a rose in its reddening a berry
in its glittering a finch in its throbbing a cowry
in its extraordinary allusiveness a night
of midsummer in its fragrance a tide
in its deepsurging and a dark woodland spring
in its concealing sources
see how it is velvety how its innerness clings
and presses how nearly it repulses
how it then takes and cherishes how it is austere
how it is free how it reviles abuses
and how it is here and how it was always here.

THE SUN

Such a reasonable irrational fellow goodhumored
and reliable too since the occasional scorching
is someone else's fault   No wonder
the ancients frankly adored him

and if their solemnity seems now simpleminded
nevertheless he is highly esteemed and honored
more than sometimes appears   A landlord
who never asks for the rent is hardly
to be despised   And what does he care for
but to be good company
with everything and to promote the common welfare
by maintaining the regularity
of public occasions   Unhappily although he desires
nothing but calm and abhors the solitary
he dwells alone burning with a million fires.

THE CHILD'S BEING

Extended and always uncentered which is why it scares
everyone but him   When an insistent finger
stabs him with a you he only stares
uncomprehendingly a stranger
to the pronominal itch and then pointing anywhere
to the tree the cloud the flower distant or near
expostulates in manic delight
me me me a spendthrift spate
of consciousness   And thus the child puts on
his being as the dark world
in its necessity puts on the dawn
by turning toward it   The child
trembling in halflight giving himself away
becomes sun's favor the choice of what is not willed
a being freeborn and intricate like the day.

THE BEING AS MEMORY

A carpet raveling on the loom a girl
with a widowspeak and misty legs a moon
like a fisheye rising from a pool
a black longwinging loon
bursting afire in the sunset a torn sail
groveling in a wave a whisper in a stairwell

.

a helmet upturned in the black rain
and later a star reflected like a coin
glimmering on seastones a sound of motors
and machineguns
in the dawn a kiss and candleflame a sonata
for clarinet a bone cracking a woman
wearing a blue veil and in kashan in a room
where the little darkeyed weaving girls lay down
and died a carpet raveling on a loom.

THE BEING AS MOMENT

Between a sea and a sea where the combers meet
in the cancellations of their endless breaking
between a dream and a dream where the night
arrests in eternal waking
between two notes of a thracian song where the flute
stops and an infinite stillness opens what
is it where is it what and where
oh sea and dream and song   Will the blurred
images surging ever fill the abyss
toward which they flow   Sighing
in the long languid tango of their kiss
will the lovers on that continually dying
wave of sensation ever really know
what they know their drift and their expiring
between a sea and a sea in the faint starglow?

THE BEING AS PREVISION

The mindseye is flitting like a moth among summer firs
the palewhite slowfast moth that threads the burning
pillars of the hidden sun and fares
tricklingly over the ferny
firesplashes of the forest bed among whorls
of misty gold rising in aureoles
under the branches   There the veeries
whistle the variations of a curious
doubling echoing note and the ovenbirds

shriek surprising hallelujahs
in unseen transepts   There the filigree ferns
the moccasin flowers the great trees
and the palewhite moth are a lucency in the semidusk
of causeless light until through a gap the source
burns burns for a dazzling instant and then turns blank.

The Ecstasy

Dawn will be the time and the forest will be the place
the brook the stone in their arrest and flowing
turning perpetually in the kind of grace
that is simply a kind of knowing
intensified around this present   The woman's face
halfsmiling against the stone will seal the force
of the lordly surging flooding sun
entering with her husbandman
entering surging flooding and yet not seen
and never to be told   The brook
its music almost lost or too serene
for her to hear will in its small crook
fold her on the stone   Her strange halfsmile
as if the earth had found its generic look
will stay upon the stone a long long while.

The Summer

Cicadas blur the ear as the blue heat haze
blurs the eye   Fulfillment is a word
known to be lucky and hence not nice
or perhaps a shade absurd
Wise folk avoid it though they may speak of days
of changing tension   Softly the hayfields rise
in the seedtime's changing browns and rusts
to the green mountain where the farthest crests
blur in purple boundaries like the child's
outreaching perceptions
and fall back in media gloria like the folds
of the woman's experience   The redwings

the meadowlarks the treeswallows zoom in the warmth
small and sudden pleasant interconnections
uniting all this knowledge with the earth.

THE NOTHING I

Look in the flower deep in the tulip cup
where the redness sinks in a still whirlwind of black
look in the stone look in the drop
of water or look back
or forward to the moon or the sun or look up
to the wells of the sky look down the hot strip
of the highway straightening forever
or in the glass gone black and silver
of the cars plunging past look in the socket
of the candlestick or in that
of the shotglass look in the empty gauntlet look
in the clamshell or in the straw hat
of the president look well in the book
whose perfect lines string out so black and flat
look at the cigarette smoke rising look look

THE NOTHING II

where the child's eyes glaze with memory where the man's glaze
with foreknowledge and how they darken and alter
to vacancy as when the shifting breeze
ramps like a closing shutter
on the deeplighted bay look in the woman's eyes
bravely in her moment of rapture when the skies
loom between her lashes or look there
in the mirror at those eyes bend closer
and closer still look in the black pupils
where other eyes appear
and in them others infinitely infinitely pools
of incomprehension look the fear
is nothing look the courage nothing the song
has no consequence look look it is here
nothing nothing nothing nothing nothing.

The Wheel of Being I

Changing figures   The dionysian child
the woman in her assurances the old town
in its hallucinations spilled
like dominoes the mountain
and the void the moon and the sun whirled
from misthidden vale to vale and the day coiled
in the forest   A word is like an ant
dragging a dead spider the meant
and the unmeant   So upon ragged changing seas
the poem which is a ship
buoyed by its hollowness on the abstruse
coordinates of meaning carries the loop
of its horizon forever with it   Scan
this circle vanishing across the deep
It is contrived it is actual it is a man.

The Wheel of Being II

Such figures if they succeed are beautiful
because for a moment we brighten in a blaze of rhymes
and yet they always fail and must fail
and give way to other poems
in the endless approximations of what we feel
Hopeless it is hopeless   Only the wheel
endures   It spins and spins winding
the was the is the willbe out of nothing
and thus we are   Thus on the wheel we touch
each to each a part
of the great determining reality   How much
we give to one another   Perhaps our art
succeeds after all our small song done in the faith
of lovers who endlessly change heart for heart
as the gift of being   Come let us sing against death.

MY FATHER'S FACE

Old he was but not yet wax,
old and old but not yet gray.
What an awkwardness of facts
gray and waxen when he lay.

Rage had held me forty years,
only five have sought his grace.
Will my disproportionate tears
quell at last his smiling face?

Awkwardly at his behest
I this queer rhyme try to make
after one that he loved best
made long since by Willy Blake.

   • • •

Cannot. In
my own way, half inarticulate,
must sing the blues.

Oh how he lay there
quiet as cast dice, crooked. They had given him
a face he never wore

smiling like anyone,
like God –
he, my own, who had smiled only

in the smear of pain,
as now my hemlock smears in this wind
dripping with half-snow, half-rain.

Smoke flares from my stovepipe,
breaks sharply down, away,
blue, whipping the leafless alders, vanishing,

while I watch from my window, this shack
in a scrap of meadow
going to woods –

alder, chokecherry, yellow birch, ash,
and the one old hemlock leaning forth,
smeared in half-snow, half-rain, November and the north.

.   .   .

Southward, downcountry
was where he lay
and I stood

in a loathsome mass of bleeding flowers
that April. Sun flashed and was gone, cold.
We two there, lashed stiff in old antagonism,

yet altered. It was that new smile
fingered on him, official, patented,
like the oil that shone on the pale oak catafalque:

such means they use to publicize, to promote
a marketable death.
He was worthy, worthy! –

I blurted, tried to blurt
in the clench of a surprise of tears.
And then my anger shifted from him to them.

In that horror
of hurting flowers
where I stood and he lay

I, frozen, was turned around inside my years
as a shadow turns
inside the changing day.

.   .   .

Why couldn't they let him be himself?
Like all our family he smiled
with a downturned mouth.

No doubt professional death-tenders are required,
competence is required, yet I wish they had let him
lie as he had fallen,

old Darwinist smiling
at the light gone down in the south,
at the leaf gone down.

Strangely, the birds had come. Already
in cold twilight robins sang,
and he heard them, the simple but rich song,

like Blake's, melodious for a fair season to come,
he heard them and he fell down,
unable to last till summer.

It was a reversal.
At the wrong time, in April, light dwindled
and the leaf fell down.

But hearts burst any time.
He took it smiling
with a downturned mouth.

•   •   •

The old Socialist!
And his father before him.
Era of eyeshades, rolltops, late tracks in a snowy street,

a flare of shots maybe in the dark,
and the talk, talk: that man eating,
this man not.

It was all so blessedly simple.
Hate, hate the monopolists!
Ah, and have I not, sirrah? –

but power of money has bought the power of heart,
monopoly eats the word, eats thought, desire,

your old companions now in the thick of it, eating —

is that betrayal? They fatten, but for my part
old hatred deepens,
deepening as monopoly deepens,

until my socialism has driven me to the sociality
of trees, snow, rocks, the north — solitude.
Strange outcome. Like so many.

I'll walk now; the woody meadow,
the firs, the brook, then higher to the birches.
I wish you were coming too.

     •   •   •

"Alyosha left his father's house
feeling more depressed and
crushed in spirit

than when he entered it . . ." I walk,
going at last nowhere
in the snow and rain

that lock in air
and nap the gray rock with gray fur.
Beside me, among the ferns that confide

their green trust to the snow,
something stalks, or seems to stalk. A partridge?
Or my mind's shadow? Minute fires flow

in the lichened rock, and a yellow eye
blinks like a shuttered lens among the ferns.
Shadows and strange fires,

who can deny them, aspects of the cold world
and the father's house? We rebel
backward, ever backward, going

behind the ancestral impositions of reality.
To seek, to find – not to impose. So we say.
But it is a sad business.

     •   •   •

Once he brought
to his blue house in the guttering chestnut forest –
oh, I remember this –

a pomegranate in his pocket.
But let me describe to you a killed chestnut tree.
Leaves, fruit, even the bark have long fallen

to the dark alien disease, and at last
the tree itself lies down
in a twisted, rising-and-falling

shape, and it never rots.
The smooth wood, pale and intense,
undulates

in a kind of serpentine passivity
among waves of witch hazel and dogwood
that wash along it

summer after summer after summer.
And so the killed chestnut has become
something everlasting in the woods,

like Yggdrasill. Tradition is not convention.
Tradition is always unexpected,
like the taste of the pomegranate, so sweet.

     •   •   •

I must complete my turning.
With purpose, very coolly, I raise my vision,
snipping

a thread of the net that holds
everything together.
My splashing fears subside about my knees.

How easy! I wonder why
I took so long, learning
that to destroy

what could never be either right or wrong,
this net, this mere order
or any order,

is no real destruction —
look, I walk as I have always walked,
one foot in front of the other foot.

The rocks and birches take so warmly
to the purity of their restoration. I see this.
I have done it with one gesture, like that.

I walk in the tact of the ultimate rebel
graduated from conspiracy,
free, truly free, in the wonder of uncreation.

      .   .   .

Well, the traditions of woods are sweet,
but something is withheld, something . . .
O my father, where is the real monopolist?

Can I, alien, avoid spreading
my dark disease? But you would say then,
seek its purity, deep at the root, radically.

If the orderly massacre of order creates an order,
then let it be new, even now, from the beginnings of things.
I am cold to my bones, my red hand clings

like a wind-plastered leaf to a white bole of birch,
the sky is speckled with snow-flecks

driven downwind, vanishing. It is all a song

vanishing down the wind, like snow,
like the last leaves of the birch
spinning away in harsh beauty. The hardhack,

clotted with snow, bends and rattles,
a sound like jeering in the driven twilight.
Why must the song be so intricate? What am I now,

what is my sorrow, has it not spun away?
Your face, snow-flecked, seems torn
downwind like the song of birch leaves.

     •   •   •

Confused darkness turns a page. Wind slackens,
cold night is beginning, in the last light
the god of winter walks, gray and alone,

Odin, Windigo, St. Malachy, someone
with a downturned smile brushing the fir boughs,
shaking the dead reeds and ferns.

Snow thickens, leaning toward the south.
Could he come home tonight
to his house, his woods, the snow, the snow-light?

My thought sings into snow, vanishing.
At least I have two clear choices: to stamp
in deepening cold, half-blind, dragging

my feet in freezing ferns, determining
my way in darkness, to the ragged meadow,
the shack with the rusty stove;

or to stay where I am in the rustle of snow
while my beard clots and whitens
and the world recedes into old purity

and the snow opens at last to the stars

that will glisten like silent histories breaking
over a silent face, smiling and cold.

        ·   ·   ·

O thou quiet northern snow
reaching southward wave on wave,
southward to the land below,
billow gently on his grave.

Snowy owl that glides alone,
softly go, defend his rest;
buntings, whirl around his stone
softly, thou the wintriest.

Gently, softly, o my kind,
snow and wind and driven leaf,
take him, teach my rebel mind
trust at last in this cold grief.

MICHIGAN WATER: A FEW RIFFS BEFORE DAWN

(In memory of Richard Wright)

I

This hour is best, darkening
in absences; loud lights quieten
in a room in a city in the West.

Hour of calm, hour of silences,
silence lingering between the beats;
hour of distances, hour of sadnesses.

Listen, the softly thinking drum
measures the silence in which the bass
murmurs to make the meaning come.

Tranquilly my fingers contemplate
the bone they are, the bone they meet —
these keys breathing among shadows.

Silence holds the sweetness in the tune.
But now who cares? Will our affection,
the great slow sound, tell anything?

Visionaries sauntering in the sound,
you ten well-drunken in dark and light,
sing well, define, dream down the land.

What in the hour, and what in the heart
of sadness, sings in the song's shadow?
Sweet silence, is it then Chicago?

2

Define. So the drum commands,
so the bass entreats. Define.
Ten black men setting out to dine.

Food of heaven had they none,
food of hell was so damned sweet
they sought and sought, and they had none.

The rope, the knife, the stone, the gun,
the train, the door, the cave, the tree,
the sign, the shutter, the snow, the dead.

Impossible to see, impossible! –
in the lake a wheel turning,
in the water a flaming wheel turning.

Like drowned rats, sodden in the dawn,
back through the streets they bring him
in dead march, the watery one.

Dawn comes to the city as to a cellar,
always gray, seeping, always gray,
and we call it, naturally, Pain of Day.

At one rotten moment of the light
the room stops, neither day nor night,
the music falters, neither black nor white.

3

My brother and I, without hope,
set forth upon the city, going
in a white cart drawn by a black goat.

The goat was singing as he must,
my brother and I were not so brave.
The sun hove, shaken in his lust.

We stopped now here, now there
at rusty doors to take upon us
Godspeed and the departing cheers.

They gave us gifts of huge sums
of money. One gave his old coat.
Another gave his old fat wife.

"Good-bye, good-bye . . ." We went on.
We were hungry. Near the airport
in a field we killed and ate the goat.

Nothing whatever happened, except
my brother who had been weeping smiled
and I who had been smiling wept.

Hence, scorched in that field, we knew
we were successful. When we returned
indeed the people gave us angry faces.

4

Listen, in night's last tender hour,
listen, the somewhat stronger beating –
Chicago, our only city, speaking.

Steel: Shall I not, my children,
grow ever brighter, stiffening
against you my abominable beauty?

Concrete: Ah, I crumble! Back
to earth, sterile, changed,
a hundred lives at every crack!

Glass: Thought you would build a
museum case to house you? True enough,
I'll gleam forever. Wait and see.

Chrome: Even I, in my tarnish,
will stay forever in my opposition
to you: I can never diminish.

Brick: Your fathers knew something of touch
and skill and excellence in shaping,
something of gratitude; but not much.

All: Wind, water, stars, and all things
hard and mindless are our company.
Make your music; the night was long.

5

My Chicago, city of all
the world, strewn
humble-jumble on a wild lakeshore.

We had at one time a beast,
a gorilla, famous among men,
and we kept it at the Lincoln Park Zoo.

In the heart of the city we had a beast
famous among men for power,
natural beauty, pride, and malevolence.

Its eyes bloomed like unlucky flowers
in a rock-cleft face, nodding in the wind
of emptiness nowhere beyond the cage.

The beast died prematurely of a heart
attack; which is to say, of fear.
And it was mourned almost everywhere.

The sun will shine in my back door
some day. But Lord the beast is taken,
taken Lord, taken and taken away.

Listen, the lake waters are seeping
in a thousand conduits, creeping
under the pavement. Listen.

6

In the cage no word is spoken,
no power of darkness
covers the eyes with forgetting.

In the cage no amnesty
waits in the government of the days,
no behoof, no behest.

In the cage no listener hears
these superb particular concussions
of blood, neither a brother nor a sister.

In the cage the moon is irrelevant,
the sun unintelligible,
and the constellations unrecognizable.

In the cage laughter is courage
and courage is laughter and laughter
is courage is laughter is — *the cage!*

In the cage knowledge is the cage
and the comfort of knowledge
is an exceedingly narrow comfort.

Days succeed and fail. What more?
Nothing, except the murmured "no"
after the clanging of the door.

7

Gray dawn seeping through stone —
see, the room blanches. Let the beat
intensify. Between bone and bone

the little blood aches with rain
and the tones deepen. Music!
Given all to Saint Harmony, all,

the pain, the awareness of the pain.
That is all. Music is heard
in one heart, harmony's great chord

in one conscience only; and yet
there is this not explained reaching,
touching, extending, as if the pain

could gather each of us to its own
being. Is it possible? The drum
murmurs against the graylight dawn,

the bass, in unison now, is calm,
the piano descends firmly. Chicago,
city of our music, the long "no,"

listen; the night was a good song;
and we are a true city, rising
in the unjust hour, honorable and strong.

THE MYTHOLOGY OF DARK AND LIGHT

THE FIRST VERSION

New England is a region of the heart
where she has lived always, artist
of Jahweh's unnameable burden! The forest

is cosmopolis. She wanders, a stranger
to its cantabile of green, knowing no
surprises, among beings who bear time

as they must, showing forth their changes,
the rapid, the slow. Sunlight and leaves
in combinations so various they might be

trivial, though they are not, make a dappling
of light and dark. She encounters,
without concern, a ruin. New England

is a region of common remains. Stone
that was hand-hewn, not quite square,
raises the lip of a foundation

on an old cellar-hole, all trace
of timbers gone. From the deep center
a birch swells, whitely tumescent

in a fringe of ferns. She is incurious
but gratified, and she looks intrepidly in,
walking around the ruin's emerging newness,

studying curves, angles, planes, a possible
portfolio. Not far away in the decayed orchard
is a well covered with two capstones,

worn granite and a chink between. She stands,
kneels, goes down with her palms
on the coolness. She stares into darkness

that is nothing but black, the whole of color,
down into the reverberating density

of all essence, meaning with no design,

to the wink of light there, glittering. It is
immensely distant, unimaginably close.
Perception floats on a pencil point

that leaves no mark, no line. When she stands
she knows the inexpressible that she has always
known, the zoom of the absolute

in resonances of delight and nausea,
the place of ruin, the place of renewal,
and she walks away in the traffic of the trees.

The Second Version

When I went looking for you
    in the place of darkness that was like a house
I came first to the voices I could not see
    in discourse of great importance
to me, to everyone
    as if I were hearing waves wash along a shore
on a telephone, having dialed the wrong number.
    There was movement, there was a smell
of stale grapefruit, coffee grounds, and wine.
    Everything seemed in one sense quite ordinary,
yet I could see nothing, nothing at all.
    The voices were serious, deliberative,
perhaps argumentative,
    and when I recognized you
(by the perfume of woodsmoke you have for me alone)
    you were reluctant to leave,
you were tense and you pretended to be shy,
    by which I knew that you would not tell me
what I failed to understand.
    But you came with me, even so.
You came behind me across stony floors
    past objects like large sponges or sharks,
the sofas and other furniture of that house,

until we arrived at the place of twilight
  where at last I could see you
    and where you could see me.
You stopped, you smiled – I think wistfully –
    and you turned back.
Since then I have stayed in this back garden
    like a furtive thief
lurking in the camouflage of the ivied wall,
    watching the light
fall on the green hills far away
    and thinking of you.

THE THIRD VERSION

Urashima, the fisher boy, was abroad on the sea
    when a girl who has no name in the story
came to his boat. So lovely was she
    that when she invited him to go with her
he went – and found himself far in the depths
    of darkness undersea, before an obscure palace
more impressive than any dwelling one can imagine.
    Urashima and the girl lived together there
for three years in untroubled happiness, surpassing
    anything he had ever known or suspected,
but then the fisher boy grew homesick.
    "All right," said the girl with no name,
"here is a sacred casket that will take you safely home,
    but only if you promise never to open it.
Promise?" "Yes," said Urashima. And it was so,
    the casket floated him safely home,
but there, amazed, he found everything changed,
    his parents dead, their house gone,
whole villages where once the fields had lain empty,
    and Urashima soon discovered
that he had been away not three but three hundred years.
    He was devastated. He went down to the beach
and looked into the ocean's darkness
    but could see nothing. Perhaps, he thought,
if I open the casket. . . . He opened it,

and at once a wisp of white smoke
came from it and trailed across the sea
and then the casket was empty.
It was a long instant, there on the bright coast
of Japan, while Urashima changed
through all the ages of man; his hair turned white
and then fell out; his belly sagged
and then grew gaunt; and for a second
he was an old man hundreds of years old.
Bright sun was on the bright sand. A shriveled
man-corpse lay like the shell of a crab.

THE FOURTH VERSION

In less than half-light
                when shadow
clings to the room,
in the late hour when darkness
flows from the forest
                to the meadow,
nevertheless a light rises
in the bone, rises also
out in the field, in the glinting
                glacial stone
that makes points of surety
in the unreliable dark.
So fine the sculptured light
                on the pillow
and the gleam out in the earth
that they seem beautiful,
as if beauty were an absolute,
                a design
in the dark unchanging depths
of light. Is it so or not?
Is it worse if the fine small light
is beauty only by inference
                of joy or praise
in the need of the night?
To have seen it is something.

Imagination can do that
            in stone or bone.
But to have raised it, roused it
            in the face
is more than imagination can do
alone. The rest is the power
most clearly ours, most human
            and the best.

THE FIFTH VERSION

His Dream

Raspberry thickets leaping, splashing
on the barrier of old stone, remnant
of a prior civilization, where she rises
with light streaming from her flanks
and stands half-turned, the she-bear
born from the oceanic earth that still
darkens her eyes;
                stands in the might
of her sex, poised, uncertain, waiting.
Then she comes to him, touches him,
rubs herself against him, and he longs
to embrace her but his limbs are wooden,
he cries out in an anguish of rustling,
his heart thuds under his ribs of bark.

Her Dream

Secret amusement, the inward smile
she cherishes alone while she walks
among huge geometric shapes,
spheres and pyramids, mile upon mile
in the glare of the intense plain.
Motorcycles race past her, ridden
by singleminded men with flames
fluttering from naked shoulders.
She steps from shadow to shadow.

Hot light and the din of motors –
how absurd. She waves to a cyclist
who gapes in amazement and races on.
In the shadow of a sphere she finds
an abandoned machine, the frame,
the wheels and handlebars, but no
motor. She mounts it, her back curved,
the smooth heaviness between her thighs,
and with a power generated inside her,
a power gratifying beyond expectation,
she glides forward, swifter than all,
in the cool wind, in the silence.

THE FINAL VERSION

It will come to be, but only when the myth
functionally ceases, of course. Dark and light.
Clear as black and white, or as day and night.
Folk wisdom always rhymes because what we call
wisdom is the mediating of opposites. Total
presence, total absence. All color, no color.
Remember, ours is the animal eye, not dark,
not light, but juice merely, merely transparency.
Further it is tempting to say that she, the painter,
sees from the dark toward the light and that he,
the poet, sees from the light toward the dark, but that
would be an oversimplification. Perhaps our trouble
is that we no longer can be satisfied
with oversimplification. One knows
such agonies, forceful conciliations! Kodály's
duo for light and dark (violin & cello, Op. 7)
(the agonies, too, of Heifetz and Piatigorsky), or
Vlaminck's Bridge at Chatou or that extraordinary
seizing-up of soul in The Road. At all events
though we struggle, and know we must struggle,
to retain our relativism, our mediating belief,
the two absolutes are unassailable. All and nothing.
Hence they resolve dangerously into one. Sometimes
god, vindictive and helpless, or destination,

the all too unmetaphysical injustice; but
for us the myth is $E = Mc^2$. Ever more difficult,
more dangerous, less satisfying, this human function
which we call consciousness. Trying to make
ends meet (and the solace of facetiæ). No wonder
so many drop out. Can one blame them? Yet each
defection brings us nearer to loss of function,
the time before and after myth, called Chaos.
"Ah," they cry out, such dear people, she and he.
"How can we continue? It is too hard. Too hard. . . ."

VERMONT

It's French, of course – our name. And I must think
(since nobody knows) the first to have uttered it
was Samuel de Champlain, an utter Frenchman;
the first as well to have seen our great green mountain;
or rather, first of the pallidly pigmented.
Yet truth to tell, not many of any color
were here before him. Meager is the word
for our prehistory; we are not rich
in relics, nor in much else, and that's a fact,
which may be why the divers kinds of diggers
prefer New Mexico and Arizona.
Well, the Algonquins lay to westward, Mic-macs
and their kin eastward, what else could Vermont,
hemmed in between two such antagonists,
ever expect to be but no man's land?
Or at best a land of passage. Warriors came,
hunters came (two who are one in nature),
came to make war and hunt and then go home,
those that survived. They didn't stay. They knew
our ponds and rivers, mountains and notches, knew
all our sublimities, yet somehow left
only their campfires smoldering into carbon
and a few skeletons moldering into garbage
for our three professional and thirteen amateur
archaeologists to ponder. But who'd ask more,
of either archaeologists or relics?
Not I. Vermont shares this much with my other
favorite country, Iceland, viz. that neither
required a dispossession for their conquest.
Iceland was there, pristine and uninhabited,
there for the taking; Vermont almost the same.
That's saying nothing, granted, for the auks,
those copperplate amiabilities who would have claimed
Iceland if they'd been asked, and nothing either
for the panthers, otters, moose, and wolverines,
and the pine trees of Vermont. What was it like,
this land of passage? Green. Remarkably green,
and not in summer only but all year round.
White pine was what the plant biologists call

our climax – nature's multimillennial orgasm –
especially on the mountains: trees as tall
as western pines, and brilliantly, brightly green.
No wonder Champlain, looking up at Mansfield
from his longboat over the windblown lake,
murmured "ver' mont" and wrote it on his map.
The best were blazed with the king's purple, to be
cut down, dragged by oxen to Otter Creek
or the Onion River or the Lamoille, and floated
into the lake and north to the St. Lawrence,
thence by ship to the royal navy yards.
Vermont white pine made the best mast in the world.
(India, Arnhem Land, have you seen our pines?)
The rest were burnt for potash. Now you'll hike
from Big Jay down to Pisgah and not see
a pine tree more than twelve rod tall. The valleys,
it's said, had plane trees (where they grow no more),
the foothills beech, then maple and butternut
on higher ground, birch by the ponds and brooks.
Et cetera. Speaking of water, maybe
the Yorkers have us beat, some say they do,
with Saranac's wild splendor. And yet, imagine
Willoughby back before the people came,
including Frost's Hill Wife (I wish I'd known her):
how the sun shone on that blue surface set
in its fringe of birch and fir, or how the mists
in early morning swirled between the cliffs
on either shore, with Wheeler Mountain dome
over beyond. I wish I'd seen it. I wish
I'd seen Vermont, the whole Vermont, just once
in that great classical time before the trees
departed, once so that I could see now
more clearly what it might have been. I know
what it is, a land of passage. Oh, there's some
who would deny it, seekers for what they call
their "roots." But when our people began to come
they never stopped, and most were passing on.
The Allens and their breed, rough frontiersmen,
rum-drinkers and free-thinkers, you can't help

liking them, and yet you can't admire them,
speculators that they were, manipulators
of timber, potash, *land*. When Ethan stormed
Ticonderoga was he the patriot? Or
was he merely defending the several thousands
of square miles belonging to the Onion River
Land Company, which he and his brothers
had founded? Later, when it seemed he might
secure their holdings through a separate peace,
it's true, negotiations were begun,
secret negotiations, obscure meetings
with Britishers in Canada, and that's how
Vermont got started, this peculiar mixture –
heroism, hardship, greed. It never stopped.
The farmers came – that's what they called themselves –
who settled the Allens' speculative miles
and plowed the hillsides up and down for corn
until the hills wore out, and then brought sheep
to graze the weeds. And when the sheep wore out,
the farmers, worn out too, their women worn out,
died or contracted a religious contagion
or moved to Nevada and started over. Others
came too, the Irish, French-Canadians, those
who thought they were in luck to work a starved
and stony land, and maybe they were. The idle,
the rich, the developers, the ski-bums, the gamblers,
they all came, seasonal migrants. They blotted out
what was left of the green mountain to make
their ski-tows, hostels, and chalets. And now
they're set to build a dog track, so I'm told,
over in Georgia Plain – a dog track! That's
whippets and hounds chasing a tin rabbit. Maybe
Vermonters need that image of themselves.
For me, I swear I'd rather have cock-fighting
than dog-racing any time. At least the chickens
do what they do without a mechanical motive.

West Bolton is due north of Bolton, East
Burke is due south of Burke, and, yes, South Reading

is three-and-one-half miles northwest of Reading.
You might say Vermonters don't know where they're at.
"What's the difference, it's all Vermont." Granted.
And so wherever we are we claim our right
to name it: Calais rhymes with palace (only
there *is* no Calais, just East Calais and
West Calais, the center having vanished). Charlotte
is pronounced shallot; Berlin rhymes with Merlin;
Ely rhymes with Swahili. I admire
our independence, so do we all, seeing
there's not much else in this world to admire.
Vermont is what you might call a Society
for Independent Mutual Self-Admiration.
We've had two presidents. Chester A. Arthur
was born in Fairfield (some say Waterville,
but Fairfield's where they've built the "replica"
of the Arthur homestead, dreamed out of thin air,
the original having burnt up or sunk down
a good while before anyone noticed, so
Fairfield is where it is), and then passed on
to York state at an early age and never
set foot in Vermont again; Vermont's loss is
the nation's gain. Then there was Calvin Coolidge,
born in Plymouth and passed on there as well,
a remarkable steadfastness. Cal at heart
was a poet, perhaps our greatest native-born poet;
it's hard to tell though, Vermont not being
notably friendly to the arts. Her sons
are channeled into other callings. Cal
went into politics and took his poetry with him.
Who else has put the whole of modern history
into one line of suitable pentameter?
"The business of America is business."
Ethan would have approved that. As for me,
I wish I'd written it, though in my spirit.
I've mentioned Robert Frost already. He
was a Californian. Everyone knows he made
a good thing out of Vermont, and Vermont
is making a good thing out of him. His place

at Ripton is a tourist attraction only
somewhat less popular than skiing and well
ahead of the Joseph Smith Monument at
Royalton. Well, perhaps I wish I'd written
"The Hill Wife" too, though mainly I'm content
to read it once a year, and then a dozen
or fifteen other poems with it. No,
I'd not be Frost. The truth is, first, that finding
an honest-to-God Yankee son-of-a-bitch
is not easy, but when you've found one, look out! –
you've found a humdinger, maybe a Robert Frost;
second, that Frost has been a frightful burden
to all younger Vermont poets, who have spent years
fighting him off, until now at last we dare
approach nearer, a little, without the fear
of losing our own identities (poetry
is poetry, after all, and Vermont's Vermont);
and third, that recently the state's become
far more hospitable to poets – oh,
mind you, not native-born (Paul Blackburn from
St. Albans had to take his splendid talent
to New York City before he found a home),
yet many of us are here. Why, in this one district,
northwestern Vermont, there's Hewitt of New Jersey,
Broughton of Pennsylvania, Bass of Texas,
Edwards of Georgia, Engels of Michigan,
Budbill of Ohio, and Huddle of Virginia –
yes, and Kinnell of Rhode Island too, I'll stick
him in, ours by right though living a trifle
eastward, Sheffield way on the height-of-land –
and all twanging away in one or another fashion
of Yankee song, and all of us passing on.
Have I been too hard on Frost? Let's say I have.
Let's say he made, out of his own bad temper
and this forsaken and forsaking land,
a large part of our context. Not the whole,
not that by any means, but nevertheless
a large part. We must come to terms with him,
or find ourselves cut off completely. Frost,

whatever else you say, possessed a saving
curiosity. That's it, he got around,
he knew this people, he explored this land;
he saw, he apprehended, he perceived,
at least at his best he did, and by God that's
seven-eighths of the battle and five-eighths further
than most of us ever get. Once Ezra Pound
told me in a letter, or hollered rather,
"Curiosity, gorbloastit, kuryositty –
thass wot I'm tawkin abaout!" So bravo.
Bravissimo. These two old enemies
had more between them, I expect, than either
would have been willing to allow. A hundred
years from now they'll almost look like friends.

I'm from Connecticut. But please, not Stamford,
not New Canaan. I'm a Litchfield man –
Litchfield County, that is – like Ethan Allen.
A speculator too? Some say I've farmed
this poetry hill for what it's worth. I could
offer extenuating circumstances,
my life has had them (and maybe not much more),
but truly now, what else could I have done,
being, or trying to be, a poet? That means a person
in the fullest sense. And does that mean in turn
something of a son-of-a-bitch? I think
Vermonters know, better than anything else,
just what a plus-and-minus tangle man is.
There was a man of Stowe who wondered which
mountain was higher, Mansfield or Camel's Hump,
until, maybe to win a bet, he climbed the peak
of Mansfield, loaded a ball without the wadding,
lay down and steadied his flintlock on a stone
and aimed at the ne plus ultra of Camel's Hump.
Sure enough, slowly the ball rolled forward
and dropped from the muzzle, a gratifying plop,
as I imagine, onto the alpine moss.
Mansfield was higher, and is, if by no more
than twenty rods. On the way down he killed

one bobcat for sport and two snowshoe hares
for the family pot. The only way I know
to do a thing is the directest way,
in art as elsewhere. (Though that's not to say
the imagination in a particular work
may not choose indirection.) Vermonters take
the directest way in everything but speech.
I knew a woman once in Beebe Plain
that had an idiot girl she kept at home
and dressed and fed and babied till the girl
was thirty-five in years and nigh in heft
to two sacks of hog ration. Bess, what for,
they asked her more than once, how come you don't
put her out with the state or in a home?
Bess'd look straight and answer, "Hell, I know
her feed's worth more than she is, which is nothing,
and that don't take in the labor – mine, that is.
I guess I'm used to her, is all. Besides,
if she wan't here who would there be to show me
how smart I am?" That's how she spoke her feelings.
It's something like our feelings for Vermont.

Those Indians who came and didn't stay,
no doubt they had their business, yet they were
in one sense tourists. Did they lay a curse
on our green mountain (like many a tourist since
who's et our beans)? Nobody would blame them,
and something must account for our obsession
with snatching dollars out of strangers' pockets.
Down in Montpelier the state development
commission spends a hundred grand a year –
which is not hay, by God – in advertising
our sleepy farmlands and our quaint red barns,
but not one cent to keep our farmers eating
or those barns standing. How can New England farms
compete with those monster western corporations?
We need a new crop, something that will grow
on hillsides, and on granite hillsides at that.
There was a fellow over in Underhill

who ranched musk oxen and proved it could be done,
but do you think the state would lend a hand?
My own idea that I've been working on
is a neat machine that will exactly crack
butternuts so the meat will come out whole.
Oh, there's a market for them. Rose Marie
knows eighteen recipes. But cracking them –
the butternuts, that is, though Rose Marie's
handwriting can be pretty near as hard –
takes hammer and anvil, and generally it means
bloody fingers and nutshells in your cookies
and a visit to the dentist. Who needs that?
Well, all I need is *half* a hundred grand.
That's all; no more. Think what the state would save.
And I'd have just enough to get me started
and work out a few bugs in my neat machine.
Then what? Easy. I'd make all Butternut Mountain
one huge farm and then hire half the town
at harvest time, which would just nicely fill
that slack, fidgety season after the cider
has been put down to work and everyone
is sitting around uptight, waiting to test it.

Republicans? We've got a few. In fact
that's damned near *all* we had for a hundred years.
Then in '64 we went for the Democrats,
the first time, went for the lesser evil
(that's what we thought) and gave our vote to Johnson
against Goldwater, and you can bet we won't
make that mistake again. Right now we have
a Democrat for governor, which isn't
a mistake exactly, it's an aberration.
I don't know if it's true, but I've been told
the poor guy suffers so much from loneliness
down there in Montpelier he has to call
a press conference just so he can find
someone to talk to. Mind, I don't say it's true.
Vermonters are Republican because
Bostonians are Democrats, that's all.

That's enough. Still there are Republicans
and Republicans. Take New Hampshire,
for instance; over there if you object
to the divine right of state senators
you're a Communist. Why hell, I knew a man
living in Coos Junction who wouldn't take
a twenty dollar bill; he couldn't stand
to carry Andrew Jackson in his pocket.
"Gimme two tens," he said. "Ain't it just like
them fathead red-tape artists? They design
the twenty for a red, then put a great man
like Hamilton on the tens." As far as I know
there's only one hereditary senator
in Vermont, and that's Fred Westphal from over
Elmore Mountain way. I don't know for sure
how Fred feels about Andy Jackson, but
he's carrying Elmore in his pocket and the rest
of his district too. Fred told a friend of mine
he'd never kissed a baby's face or a voter's
ass. I expect that's right. Of course it's not
exactly saying what he has done either
to keep himself down there in the legislature
since God knows when. "He's drawed his pay and 'tother
perquisites" – that's what my neighbor says.
My neighbor's an anarchist. That is to say,
a Vermonter, and that's to say, a Republican.
But just because he goes by the same label
as Nelson Rockefeller doesn't mean the two
have anything in common. They're worlds apart –
worlds. Ask my neighbor how he feels about
the government – the State with a capital S –
and what comes back is pure Bakuninism,
only of course with due allowances for different
times, places, idioms, and temperaments.
"Sons-of-bitches, every one of them" – that's
his feeling, and he means Rockefeller too,
or maybe especially. Why, I suspect
even Fred Westphal might be an anarchist,
though he'd turn the color of Ed Wipprecht's

best red cabbage if you accused him of it.
For my part, what's the use of stalling? I'm
an anarchist, have been for forty years,
only more a Warrenite than Bakuninite,
which is to say, nonviolent and independent,
or in other words American, which is what
lets me remain a patriot and a son
of the Founding Fathers, like my friend Paul Goodman –
Paul, the city Jew-boy who worked and fought
in New York all his life, fighting for virtue
or even for reason in an evil, crazy city,
and lost, and was always losing, which was why
he liked the country maybe and called his poems
hawkweeds and died three summers past – no, four –
over in Stratford underneath Percy Mountain.
The point is, there's a losing kind of man
who still will save this world if anybody
can save it, who believes . . . oh, many things,
that horses, say, are fundamentally preferable
to tractors, that small is more likable than big,
and that human beings work better and last longer
when they're free. Call him an anarchist,
call him what you will, a humanist,
an existentialist, hell, a Republican – names
are slippery, unreliable things. And yet
call him a Vermonter. That's what he is.

I don't say you can't find him in New Hampshire,
or even Maine – or Australia, for all I know –
the loser, the forlorn believer, the passer on.
But old Vermont is where I've found him mainly,
on the green mountain – on the western slope of it
if you want to be particular – where we talk
with that strange dialect which isn't exactly
Yankee, nor exactly anything else either.
"Calful" we say (as in *calf*), not "cahful,"
certainly not "careful," and what we make
our livings on, milking them morning and night,
are "kyeous." O.K. The further point is this:

we are still here, although we're passing on.
You won't hear much about us, but we're here.
I think we are the last true regionalists,
or maybe — who knows? — the first of a new breed.
Not local colorists, at any rate, not keepers
of quaintness for quaintness's sake. We're realists.
And realism means place, and place means
where we are. We name it, with all its garbage
and slaughter, and its comeliness too, and then
it is our center — where we are. We try,
in our own unobtrusive way, to make it
a center of everywhere, a center *for*
everywhere (and thanks to Ted Enslin of Maine
for saying that). I think and I do believe
we know the way to glory, or to what can be
glory for this worn-down bedraggled race —
peace, freedom, losing, and passing on. And place.
We know it if anyone would listen. Most likely
anyone won't. Anyone never has.

Well, I've said that Robert Frost had curiosity
and took the trouble to go and satisfy it,
on foot or driving that bay mare of his;
he saw the state, he met the people. Yet
my guess is that he traveled by himself.
Your typical Vermonter is a man
of, say, sufficient winters, or a woman
for that matter, walking the back roads,
the pastures, woodlots, hills, and brooks, alone
or with a dog, mostly looking down.
Curiosity? Yes, but it bears inward
as much as outward, maybe more. My dog
is Locky, a mixed-breed bitch, though shepherd
predominates, and in her eleven years
Locky and I have walked these thousand acres
ten thousand times, I reckon. Do you think
we go on sniffing the same old rabbit trail,
examining the same old yellow birch
forever? We grow stiff. We plod now, I

with my stick, Locky with her lame forepaw,
and mostly we look down. And so did Frost.
Which brings me to the "all-important question."
What is the difference, now at last, between
the contemporary and the archaic? I
say "drawed" for "drew" and "deef" for "deaf" and still
use "shall" and "shan't" in ordinary conversation
like any good Vermonter, and sometimes too
I write "thou" for "you." So am I therefore
dead? That will come soon enough. Meanwhile
my language is mine, I insist on it,
a living language as long as it is spoken
by living men and women naturally,
as long as it is used. And so with manners,
styles, attitudes, the whole spectrum of appearance.
As for the unappearing, the soul, what further
need or can be said? It is my own.
No, I believe this difference was concocted
in New York City, that necropolis,
city of critics and city of fashion, which is
saying the same thing. It is a place to stay.
But genuine regionalism is not fixation,
not in either sense; it is awareness
of passing on. I don't speak paradox,
I speak for once directly. Place is the now
which is eternal. And we are passing on.
The name of our green mountain is from French,
but sometimes, ungallicly, we twist it, saying
Vêrmont with the stress up front. We intend
no harm and only characteristic disrespect.
Once when I heard it I was struck by how
the name might be divided differently,
Vermont, the Worm of Being. We are torn
here in this place that is our now between
its beauty and its depravity. The beauty
is mostly old, our mountains and our farms,
and the depravity is mostly new.
We don't hate it exactly, being not
the hate-conceiving kind, but we despair.

God, we despair! – Vermont's protracted gloom,
our end-of-the-winter desolation, April
in our cold hearts. From this we make ourselves,
remake ourselves each moment, stronger, harder,
with our own beauty. Yes, our great green mountain
is the worm of being, long and irregular,
twined lengthwise through our state, our place, our now.
Meanwhile we dream of other sunnier places.
Myself, I'm going down next month to look
at a house I know of in New Mexico.

THE SLEEPING
BEAUTY

1

Ich hab' mein' Sach' auf Nichts gestellt.
— Johann Wolfgang von Goethe

Out of nothing.

This morning the world was gone;
Only grayness outside, so dense, so close
Against the window that it seemed no season,
No place and no thought almost,
Except what preys at the edge of thought, unknown;
But it was snow. The flakes, extremely fine
And falling unseen, still made the bough
Of the hemlock whiten. Here and now —
Twig by twig, needle by needle — a plume
Reached through the grayness,
Intricate purity that somehow could assume
Its own being in its own space,
Out of nothing . . .
                    or out of a cold November
Dawn that anyone could see, this grace
That no one can ever quite remember.

2

Then from beyond, from nowhere, from the wilderness,
As in a little dance stirring the hemlock plume,
Comes wind. And out of silence
Words gather.
                    Within the room
The inhabitant looks out, unknown, unseen,
A presence gathering.
                    So this pure loveliness
Of the moving air, unseen equally,
Is truly the world's breath, truly
The spirit, invisible and from nowhere,
                                        though it moves
The hemlock's whitened branch

In slow swaying rhythms that are real and proves
For every beholding this actual dance,
This beauty, which is also love.
                                        Alone
Consciousness gathers, a nothing, silence that chants
Unheard in the room, a poem made
                                        slowly
                                                by no one.

                    3
As movement seen, so is the sound, the singing,
Heard; wherefore a tremulous hope has ever
Down dim centuries sought the joining
Of these two powers together
In efficacy, in the world, in concrete meaning –
Hope forlorn now, which can be no beginning,
For the word is silent, and the word within
The word is silent . . .
                                Oh, begin
In all and nothing then, the vision from a name,
This Rose Marie Dorn,
Woman alive exactly when the Red Army came
To that crook of the Oder where she was born,
Woman who fled and fled in her human duty
And bore her name, meaning Rose in the Thorn,
Her name, the mythologos, the Sleeping Beauty.

                    4
Three persons are here, of whom the first
Is *you*, dear princess, you who are always sleeping,
Thou therefore addressed –
Thou in thy quiet-keeping –
As if immutably; and yet you dream. You rest
And you dream this world. You are mystery. You exist.

Second is *he*, the prince. He lives
Wherever and whenever he perceives

Himself in your dreaming, though in fact he is awake
And so knows the horror of being
Only a dream.

Third is the poem, who must make
Presence from words, vision from seeing,
This no one that uniquely in sorrow rejoices
And can have no pronoun.

Last, as in all dreaming,
Is heard the echo of coincidental voices.

5

You there. Your eyes hooded, shrewd a little,
Feminine always.
Remember how you lay
Shadowed in your name, naked in your beauty,
Waiting? Could you say
For whom (as he came to you), or for what encounter?
Was it yes, no, despair or hope? Or nothing?
Mortal
And eternal in mortality, Rose,
Named the Dornröschen, Princess
Of the Briar Rose, were you dreaming of *him,*
Our *history?*
Holy
Breath of creating love and harmony and time,
O Spirit,
she sleeps. How insecurely
Words try her momentous dreaming. Let the song
Sing, from that inward stress, this world so surely
Created in her sleep,
this beauty in its centuries of wrong.

6

Your dream:
His name was Homer. He was blind.

He had *gone blind* – so your dream tells you. Sight
Of the human brutality of mind
Put out his eyes, a light
Drowned at the beginning, he then confined
To dimmest story, as to its powers resigned:
How once upon the wall of Priam's
City, between the swarming armies,
Walked (and you dream the dust on her bare feet)
A woman tossed up there
By breaking waves of men heaving in heat,
In rancorous, fecund, Asian air,
The fury of romance. Surging, resurging, wet
With blood and the seminal ooze, they broke that fair
Goddess and queen. Her name was Helen. Yet

7

Was she the innocent? Too beautiful for that,
Already in time's dawn too washed with the lurid
Sunstreakings of romance, she had caught
The coupling habit, torrid
Duplexities of love and death (or fact
And fancy, real and ideal); then she grew fat
And in her old age called out the names
Of men that scorched her throat, those flames
Blind Homer saw. No, innocence was his
Whom Homer called not brave
But more than brave, who in the world that is
Knew himself victim, dead to save
The stupid heroic pride of the prime defector
In history, and still went out and gave
His life without hope or despair. His name was Hector.

8

Recurrently he also dreams:

                  A girl, seventeen, fair
Complexioned, black hair in a widow's peak,
Black eyes. French-Canadian. Her bare

White slender body seeks
Him down the years, the decades, with that bright flare
Of blood at her thighs, an emblem, and her stare
Is hooded but accusing; yet how
Can he make amends? He takes her, slow
And very gentle, joining himself to her wound
That he did not, could not, give,
Loving her completely so that no sound
Escapes him. Again and again to live
Only for her in his humility, her blood – flame
Burning him. Again and again her fugitive
Glance at him, hooded eyes always the same.

      9
As Doctor Peter said:
                    "Dreams of a menstruating
Woman may often mean a castrated man,
Your need to dominate him. Screwing
The girl is your oedipal vanquishment
Of your father, his un – manning."

                                 Shock. Undoing
The dream. Oh, not the father – maiming, crude
As it seemed, but rather the shattering
Of his dream – mood, all that mattered,
The loving and lovingkindness, the steadfastness
In existential sorrow,
The hard and human need to share – all blasted.
Could he accept it?
                  Sorrow, sorrow,
The deeper wound in loving.
                          That it was force,
Power, even in the giving, this was his sorrow.
He was man, *a* man, flawed in his very source.

      1 0
Your dream:
                  His name was Hero, and his other name

Was History
                emerging from the mists   your maker
Whom you made, your dream who came
With his sword for his scepter.

And from his right hand sprang understanding both of time
        and of fame
And his gorgeous brawn was only gentleness a peace in
        Cockayne
And in the cities of the mist, stone rising
On stone
        and the pennons flying.

The sword that was scepter changed to a pipe of song.

His name was Hero/ was History/   was He/
Ego in all its radiance come from a long
Distance across the unknown sea

Shining/
        for he carried death in his left hand death in his eyes
And from them fashioned love, both the look and the gift,
        compassionately.

And your dream made him.
                        He was yours and he was wise.

        I I
Your dream:
                His name was Herod. No? How close
In the T V's little window he comes, smiling
Into your privacy, he with his nose
So uglily beguiling
Like a lover's. You know somehow this shows
His power, his personal sympathy. He avows
The national interest and your own safety
In this new administrative program, so weighty

A decision, and he sighs for the infants smothered
(Practically painless) to avert
"Our peril." Where did he come from? He has hovered
On the screen for years, the tie, the shirt
Always impeccable. Galatian? Greek? Jew?
Who knows? A politician. Some provincial upstart
Willing to do what nobody else would do.

12

"We thought the château was safe. The men were gone,
Of course, all except Uncle Hypolyte
Half dead with dropsy. *They* came in the dawn
And took us without a fight –
Naturally. And then they chose me. Roughly, 'Come on,'
They said, 'you're the prettiest.' Out over the lawn
In my bare feet in the cold dew,
Pushed, dragged, flung to the avenue
Of old beeches,

                    where at the biggest I was bound.
And they spread my feet wide
And nailed them with whittled pegs to the ground
And built a slow fire of twigs inside
My skirts and fed it until I was aflame.
'Eh, damsel, how like you this for fucking?' one cried.
God, it was almost a kind of ecstasy when it came!"

13

Your dream:
            His name was Hesiod, a darkish man
Filled with goodness, both of the earth and the gods
(For in those days these two were one),
Who still was litigious and made
Lawsuits against his brother, and was murdered then –
For his goodness? The dream is inexplicit. Down
Rows of millet in a shining field

He walks, upward among the fig trees
Where someone with a club springs out. That's it.
He knew how far it was
(Being a poet) to Tartarus: the distance a brazen bit,
Falling below ground, would traverse
Equal to the fall from sun to earth. And so he fell.
He gave you works and days, gods of the universe,
And was murdered, and you wept, and he went to hell.

      1 4

Your dream:

         His name was Hannibal, i.e., by Baal's
Grace. Baal, god of locality. And on Alpine ridges
Where Baal dwelt he marched his incredible
Elephants, and down the edges
Of Italia fighting, yet loved by many, by all
The ordinary people, for justice, so that Africa
Might have come to Europe, new
Light in the dark of Roman law,
Nor for justice alone but leniency, the human idea;
Yet Rome prevailed
And has always prevailed, and drove him to Syria,
Crete, Bythnia, always exiled,
Always!
      Wandering grace of the native god,
Place to place passing, lost light in the field
At night, candle in history, moving toward your bed.

      1 5

Called him "Big Joe" yes and Joe Turner it was his name
And he sang yes he sang
         well them deep down country blues
With a jump-steady and a K.C. beat   that came
From his big old heart and his bouncing shoes
From that big old bouncing voice

Baby, you so beautiful and you gotta die someday

the same

As those Kansas City nights   huge boozy flame
Of the miserloos and the careless joys/   But slow
He could sing it too when it took him   sorrow
In the bone   slow

> *Brokin the ten commanmint,*
> *Beat out with the jinx,*
> *Cain't sometimes*
> *Git water to drink,*
> *Ain't got a mount to jack in,*
> *Cain't produce a dime,*
> *I'm jus' as raggdy*
> *As a jay-bird in whistlin' ti –*
>> *ime. . . .*

over and over

In the gathering of souls the flickering
Of human destiny that sways to discover
Happiness in fate.   And it was music, music.
"Shouter," they called him. And great is what he was,
Warm and   reckless   and accurate and   big –

Saint Harmonie,
      touch thou these lines with Turner's voice.

I 5

There where pines darken the water above the brookbed
Rita beckoned, pointing down to a woman's face
She had put there, "Because," she said,
"This is a secret place
And one cares for disposing of what one's made,
Even the failures." In half-relief the head
Looks upward through rippling water,
Askance, half turned back, caught
As if by its origin in the earth again.
There, beneath the waterflow

And changing reflections, pine trees, sun, and rain,
A face, although people come and go
And Rita has gone and the secret is all that stays,
As the presences of the poem alone can know,
A woman's face looks up from the water, always.

17

Oaks and dark pines, remote, the northern forest.
What does the woman's face in the water mean?
Traces of snow. This the oldest, the purest,
Naiad alive in the stream,
Ophelia drowned in eternity. She nearest
And most distant, coldest, stillest, dearest.
Crystals gleam in the brown leaves
Without sunlight. Mythological lives
Exist in dreams. Leaves twist and turn in the current,
Drift over the face and on.
Passage and change obscuring the eternal moment.
The feminine in a face of stone
Unchanged, there in cold water, the face of sleep.
Wind in the pines. Dream sound. Snow. Alone.
Woman. Forever. Water. Watching. Deep.

18

"'Thee knows. Must thee not knowe?' I so saying
Evere & againe, but onely within my Minde,
Whenso he Snorreth, after his *Plaieing*
That him so gratifieth;
Then creppit I to Candel, softlie, praying
(Mine *Blasphemie!*) the Quille not scritch, bewraying
Mine Hande in th' Colde; I tho't Godd
Griev'd not of my Scriving. What!
Cou'd I not helpe mee? No. Twas him I feart,
A Manne, wou'd hee not see
Oure Candel shorten'd? Once hee upsterted
From Sleepe & lookt wide-eied at mee,
But seeth not. Mine owne pretties, on his olde Sermons

Wrot twixt the lines — now fownd! 'Mistris, be thee
Simple?' & hee laied them, babes, to th' fier burning."

       1 9
He said:
            All right then, I *was*, o.k.? Screwing
My father. Sticking it to him for all he'd done
I know it. Can I refuse
To know? Dominion
Is sweet, revenge sweeter, and who's
To say either or both couldn't produce
A dream's gratifications? Let
Pleasure defend itself. And yet . . .

What I remember is still so very much more
Than pleasure, or even
Than love's gravest working, for it was my pure
Concern. The given
Was her hurt and her womanly sense of wrong.
What I gave was what can never be proven,
Myself, nothing, to be used by her, to belong

       2 0

To her, to *be* her, that her hurt and wrong be mine.
It was love, yes, but love rarified, burned
In the crucible. And so it has always been.

Has it? To be concerned,
What does that mean — only pity? And then
What's pity if not dominion
In another style?

            O Spirit,
Spirit of love inhabiting
Dark places of cities and bright places
Of the countryside, what
Is human meaning, what are those faces

Turned to one another? Is not
His loving more than the mere energy it seems,
A struggle to prove himself? He had thought
He could help you,
                          wounded girl of his dreams.

            2 1
Spirit
        let there be even in the last hour
Even in the scorching of the air
                                a song of love/
Spirit
        this is their only power
All that they can perceive
Of their human being   their only invention   the flower
Of consciousness/

    [Brother Estlin, he misjudg'd thee & thou'rt
Unforgiving.]

            What they have made
Is this invisible   in the void
Of visibilities, of animal vacancy
                                the bones
That snarl the stars that gnash
The trees in their imperturbable march like lions
Home from the kill/
                Out of the wash
Of the tides of essence licking their wet souls
Wearing them away
                they made this
                        hush
Of existence
        love perdurant
                        a harmony
    as of the flight of many gulls.

22

Your dream:

His name was Hölderlin. Ah, name, name!
Syllables gliding in Teutonic rhapsody
From classic order to the sweet insane,
As he in his *Abendphantasie*
Soared, his soul among rosy clouds. When the flame
Of heaven faded, when in eloquent twilight he came
Back to the garden, to you, the best
Was that darkening – ach, an Weltschmerz
Leidend, the tenderest passion. He knew that gothic tower
Deep in a forest standing,
So beautiful, so old, created in mind's power
To outlast the mind. And he knew heartrending,
The gravest and purest of loving. Beauty was worth
Its every sorrow, mind's fading or world's ending,
As darkness covered the garden that is the earth.

23

"Good-bye," they always whisper, "oh God," clinging –
And he walks down the steps in early lilac light
And she drives off in her Volkswagen
Into the snow-curtained street
And he turns and raises his hand by the elevator
And she clings sobbing and desperate at the stone gate
And he looks back in the autumn haze
From a distance under the yellow trees
And she finds his dear stinking pipe left on the bookcase
And he writes a letter
Ten pages long and tears it up and mails a postcard
And "Good-bye."
                    "Good-bye."
                                "Good-bye."
                                            Never

Shall they meet again.

Good-bye whispered, murmured,
                                        furled
In the creative wind,
                    incredible cosmic command
                                        to sever,
Disjoin, separate, break –
                    death in the world.

        2 4
You are the dreamer who dreams the world, and yet,
Princess, the world dreams you. There is never
A beginning. You create and are created,
Legend forever,
The lore of all human being, the victim who begets
Victimization; and your heroes, those who wait
For your invention, love and destroy you
As you will, you who can have no will –
Naked, spelled, fixed in the storm and flood
Of civilization, the bound
Of thorny fire, the wall of the bloom of blood.
You are known and you are never found.

Spirit, she is the vortex. Placidly she sleeps
While the heroes run impeccably round and round
About their business. Only the poem weeps.

        2 5
He thinks how, often when his semen spews,
It feels like blood. A hot leakage, burning.
How awkward! He remembers the Hindus –
Do not they wake in mourning
Invariably, their seed unrenewable? They choose
Each night between loving and dying. Then she – does
It burn her, too? Are we joined,
Victim-lovers, everyone, in this wound
Of fire forever? Do all men feel their lives

Taken in the heart of love?
Does it mean something? Anything?

                                    Thus he contrives
Enigmas from horror. He would prove
That the simplest human realities unfold
Mysteriously, and that in this knowledge he may move
Without change. Yet daily he sees himself grow old.

            2 6

You lay there on that couch as if in effigy
(How do women get out of their clothes so fast?)
Or as if an emblem, not at all stiff,
But quiet, luminous, composed,
Or so it seemed to him, your arms by your sides,
Legs straight, hair flowing around your face,
Your eyes lidded and your lips
Formed in the merest smile, nipples
Erect. The cloth beneath you, heavy brocade
Of shaded purple and gray,
Might have been stone. He looked. Were you awaiting
A transfiguring or a violation?
You did not, you probably could not, say. The moment
Was its momentum.
                        Was this then why you lay
So still? He trembled, touched near his own torment.

            2 7

Wind in the pines, a dark, damp, Novemb'ring wind,
And here with small, small song the redpolls flittering,
Branch to branch, maybe nine of a kind,
And here an oak leaf skittering
Down the cold brook, its brown curl holding nine
Grains of new snow, maybe you and your almost divine
Eight sisters quarreling to your lover,
Cold Orpheus, where he waits; and over
The brook maybe your small, small souls flit on

Cheeping their quarreling song
Per una selva oscura, downstream and down
The humid wind, your boat sailing along,
A curled brown leaf of oak, nine new grains of snow,
Past the stone face of the lady of water, sung
Through these dark woods by nine little birds as you go.

2 8

Why dost thou tear me? Had I done thee hurt?
For my name you took me
                              which was Lilith.
                                              Cunt
Was my name, the sweet thing wild & furtive
On the grass plain and the mountain.
Woman was my name.
                    Perché mi scerpi?
With the moon I was
                    and the lion
                                  and you tore me,
You uprooted me in your lust
Of enviousness and you beat down my breast
As you beat down unripe fruit from the olive bough,
You made my womb broken
And I walked in pain.
                          Lilith I was. Now
I am the pain-walker, the all-taken,
But Lilith I was. I was.
                    Perché mi scerpi?
There
        only my cry is left
                              like wind in the bracken.
Here
        I am death. You made me. Now
                              why do you tear me . . . ?

2 9

Late. The back road "slicker than owl shit." Snow

Packed hard under new powder. No tracks;
No one has been this way. Then the doe
Leaps into the headlights, a fixed
Snow-dripping instant. The truck fishtails, slews,
Spins, a great rounding out of control
And over the left bank, Jesus, backward
Into the ravine; a crunch, a lurch.
Five thousand pounds of metal too heavy to crush.
Almost slow; a wrenching.
Silence. Lights out. Damage. Disgust. Push
The door upward, its weight in this dimension
Unknown before. The doe had been small; her hoof mark
Will trail to gnawed fur this winter. Slip out, clenching
For the drop. Groan. Crawl upward through the dark.

30

Upward through the dark, this . . .

                          this non-entity
Moving from the objective crash in pained ascension
To surpass the disaster of identity,
To seek the greater intention,
Greater energy, greater coherence, a supra-entity
In a free existence, the completed person in personality,
Out from the bondage of blood and nerves,
Beyond history, between the stars,
Pure subjectivity in its spirit, its spiritual
Outreaching and inreaching,
For which no ceremony of love, no ritual,
No convention, and no teaching
Can suffice, but only love transcendent in the wreck
Of the determinant world, love continually searching
Beyond love,
    the poem crawling upward through the dark.

31

Your dream:

        His name was Hermann, tender, quiet,

Suffering, he who in his dream dreams you,
Dreaming. All fuses. Your eternal night
Is alive with stars, with moons,
With moving lanterns, shapes of Walpurgis light
Elegantly frightening, terrifying. And yet
Strains of harp-playing, Mozartiana,
And words, half-heard, of far hieratic
Resonances fill your fear with love,
Shy love by a northern
Expanse of water where the sea eagles rove
On strange incongruous winds. Thorns
Darken your dreaming. He is Hesse, he is mystery,
Steady and blue, lover, *die Polare, der Nordstern.*
All confuses. Death & love. Music & cruel story.

3 2

Blizzard in the mountains. Dusk. The cabin's light
Pales in these sheets of snow flung peak to peak,
Crag to crag, the essential might
Of everything. What's one weak
Lamp?

      A paradox. That in a wild night
Self alone through self to self can sight
Ego's perilous voyage, to sustain
Freedom and being finally in the dawn
Beyond ego.

       So the great determinant winds,
Mindlessness of the universe,
Wrack the cabin, and the boards crack and the mind's
Timber with them. Worse, it is always worse,
It is never better.

      Ahi! Who art thou, *lo buon
Maestro?* And hast thou forever gone?

        What course
Shall the voyager plot now, unguided, alone?

33

The point is (maybe) that the woman's face was *made*.
Rita made it. Then because it was (she said)
Flawed, she placed it in the brook, conveyed
It there, the woman's head
Looking up forever (almost), serene and sad.
Out of earth it came, in Rita's hands created,
In Rita's ecstasy: *out of herself*
She made it. Thus it is thought and feeling –
A meaning. And if none of us can say quite what
It is and none can say quite all,
Still it is there, our meaning mystery in the water,
Our eternity, both less and more than awful
Timelessness and nothing. It is what we make of them,
Our mythic soul (dear Rita's) against the flowing
Water, which really is forever and mind-forsaken.

34

The poem moves north.
                    "Good-bye."
                                        "Good-bye."
                                                            North

In dark dawn to Vermont, snowflakes drifting
Among the pines, a pickup, a Ford
¾-ton, F-250,
4-wheel-drive, rusty green with one door
Crimped shut forever and a busted gear
Banging in the front axle.
                    "Good-bye."
(O God, clinging.)
                    North means the way –
Bearing this image, Susan, the slight girl
Beneath great trees
Standing half-turned, head bowed, a swirl
Of yellow hair.
          "Good-bye."
                    The windshield

Fogs in the cold and the snowfall thickens. North
Means the way, loneliness, a snow-blurred field,
Existence, seeking what a life is worth

3 5

In the exigencies of consciousness,
Of language, – the poem moving.

In Argyle
Out front of the American Legion post
Is an old tenpounder with a pile
Of cannonballs, the usual pyramid, but cased
In metal strapping bolted to a concrete base
So no one can steal them.

Remember
When people didn't steal things?

Damned
If I do. But anyway I mind when they didn't
Bother with nothing small.
Railroads more likely.

Who's that?

They wan't hidden
Neither.

But who is that talking?

Hell,
I seen when they hijacked the will of the people

– Who? Who? –
Like it wan't no more than a barrel of spruce oil.
You know it same as I do. Call me Amos.

You?

3 6

You, Amos? But you're dead now.

There's a many
Will say so.

You burned out in that schoolbus
You were living in, up on Stannard Mountain.
The warden told us.

Cuss

The warden.
But he found your body.

Maybe. Maybe

It were a doe I had, for eating purposes. But mainly
In my condition you can't hardly tell
What's fact and what's a story.

Well,

What is your condition?

Nobody knows.

Nobody?

You. And you always said
You ain't nobody. Correct me if I'm wrong.

O.K.,

But you must be somewhere.

Dead. All dead,

Me and mine. Or just for the hell of it let's say
I got me a little trailer now, a place to hide
The upper side of Bear Swamp off Wolcott way

37

Back of Budbill's where it dreens offn the ledges. Snugger
Than a cat's ass in them balsams there. You won't
Locate it easy, no sir.

The truck

Slows, slips into the slant
Of a roadside turn-off. Silence and the shock
Of stopped motion. Nothing moves. Except . . .

Look

There, twenty feet off, that dead elm
With the broken branch. See that owl?
A great horner too, sitting so still the snow
Has draped him. Only
His yellow eyes, blinking once, give him away
In the soft gray snowscape.

Hungry

Cuss, ain't he? Hunting by daylight. Blind
As a cow in a barnfire. Have to be mighty lucky

To catch a meal that way, seem's-zo. I mind

38

When them old hooters had plenty eating material
Round these parts, and other folk too. Course
That were times gone. You could prevail
With but fourteen head of cows
Then, if you had the makings.

                              Makings?

                                        What I call

Makings of a man. And that means straight out all
The time, with childern on the way,
A orchard, garding, a fair stand of hay,
Pigs, chickens, you know – what we meant by farming
In those days. It's all changed now.

Last night's empties spill from a broken carton
Still glittering under thin snow
Where there's a faint yellow pattern, somebody's name
Written in urine.

                    Northward now.

                                  Past old houses,
Farms fallen, or some still working, pride and shame

39

Mingled, windows stuffed with grainsacks, "Lots
For Sale" nailed to the dooryard maple. Or past
Rich men's farms, "shelters," only not
For them, more for their taxes –
Painted houses, barns upright, then the paddocks
With matched Belgians bred for show, too big to work,
Too feisty to handle, pawing the snowy
Turf with elephantine hooves.

                              Amos,

You there?

          Where?

                Anywhere where you can hear.

Listen. In a pine forest
Downcountry, in a secret place, not far, in a clear
Smooth – running brook, there's a face. It's
A woman, Amos. Always there, always looking
Up through the water.

                    I know. Goddamn it, yes,
I knowed afore you was thought of – her lurking

      4 0

Down there like. Maybe not the same, of course.
But I seen her, God's truth, and more than once.
Even in Big Bear Swamp where the water's
Blacker than the innards of a crankcase
I saw her, by Jesus, so I backpaddled like crazy,
And when them ripples cleared off there she was,
Down in the watergrass, just as plain, as calm –
Like she was laying out somewhere in the rowan
At blackberrying time.

               Who is she, Amos?

                       Come on,
Who do you think, for Christ's sake!
Who do you think, Amos?

                 Hell, a woman,
THE woman – that's all.

             Asleep or awake,
Amos?

       Both.

         Who knows her, Amos?

                Them that come
Where I come from.

         In all this does she make
Any difference, Amos?

            Yes. I reckon. Some.

      4 1

He reads there, only a boy, fifteen, in the dingy
Corner of the library where he has found these books,

The forgotten ones, perhaps the forbidden,
Bakunin and Johann Most,
Emma Goldman and that dearest of all princes,
Piotr Kropotkin. He reads as he has not since,
Engrossed. And then he walks out in the night,
Going where warm house-lights
Gleam in repeated patterns across the mist
And rain; dismayed, in wonder
Of these rich houses. Like a somnambulist
He walks in a trance of compassion. Under
The dripping trees he pauses, he considers pain,
Pain everywhere, pain forever, the cosmogonal blunder,
And his little tears fall down in the great rain.

4 2

"For fifteen years he never knew I never
Came. The jerk. I faked, but anyone could have told.
At last, 'Maybe it could be better,'
I said. 'Why don't we go
To one of those counselors?' and we did. Then after
A spell we stopped. That was in '65. It's later
Now. It's goddamn '75, and two years ago
He 'came out,' as he called it, he went gay,
And I'm – so soon, would you believe it? – I'm in menopause,
And I don't feel so good,
And no matter what, the diet, the exercise,
I don't age nicely. Too much droop –
Chin, breast, belly, ass. He said I should forget.
And I said what the hell's the use. I sit on this stoop
In this same old chair where grandmother used to set."

4 3

His dream:
                He is dressed in a white sheet, riding
Hellbent on a bicycle down a straight white road
Between snowbanks brilliantly high and wide,
And his belly is brilliantly broad.

And the hospital, when at last it comes in sight,
Is a disused railway station, empty inside
And cold; but the birth is easy, a mere gush
Or a happy purging, and behold! in the flash
Of newborn radiance is a beautiful translucent child
With huge eyes like sapphires
And hair of streaming yellow flame; and he is wild
With joy, joy, joy, the stars
On the ceiling are shining and chiming like bells,
The snow is dancing, the trees a triumphal chorus,
Because he has done it at last,
                              the real thing,
                                        he has done it himself!

        44
Your dream:
                He was name was Hilarity but he never laughed,
Your average mimic, your stumblebum storyteller,
Poet, etc., "well acquainted with death,"
Th' apparition i' th' mirror,
On whom alone he smiled; his ally, his grotesque.
Who else had taught him all his comic craft –
Despair and terror? So with bedpan irony
He made bones out of chestnuts. Sly?
God, they broke up, holding their sides in horror,
Gagging, the mirthful mortals!
His asides were held the gallstones of his era.
Famous he was. More than that, exalted,
The top banana, honored for his Sisyphean demeanor
And after-dinner epitaphs. He upsets you, no? Yet all told
He may be your dream's key figure, the anti-dreamer.

        45
Death, he thinks. In fact he has thought it every day
For fifty years, and every night, though someone had told him
It would grow easier. But no.
                No.

                                                    Will they
Come then to help him, hold him,
All nine as he has always known them, to play
At last in that ending now not far away,
Together as he has always believed them,
The company of love in a final cohesion,
A final rapture? For concord was his assumption
Always. But no.
                    No,
They will not come. His dream of the company
Of love, of its benevolence and openness
And lovingkindness and freedom, freedom, is only
A dream. They will not come, they will not come.
And he will die, like everyone, stupid and alone.

          46
Wind sighing, crying, singing in the pines. Who knows
How to interpret the song? The snow falls
Thick or fine, altering the forms
Of land-imagery but clarifying
In water, this moving crystal above the charmed
Obsessive image. A woman's face looks upward
Always; in drapery now, for ripples
And swirls of sand have silted a little
Against her, and a few oak leaves have collected
For her décolletage.
She is half-taken by nature, she is half-accepted.
And so, half-turned to her shoulder, she gazes
Always upward, forbearant, unchanging. Memory
Knows her. In all her repetitions, image on image,
She gazes from time beyond time, from poems
                                    deep in the poem.

          47
Half-turned, as if reluctant, the lady of water
Looks upward always, yet with gaze averted,
Gentle, unadmonishing, but grave, caught

In the changing but still eternal
Flow of crystal, between air and earth, thought
And intuition, but caught there, the margin unsought
But secret, not one sphere or the other;
There and also most distant, farther
From this than Isis or Inanna, and yet clear,
Or almost but not completely
Clear, in the reflecting crystal, the lady here,
Lady of paradox, drowned and alive, obliquely
Staring from darkness into the world of light,
Held in the crystal, held there proudly and meekly,
Staring, there always,
                              even in the dead of night.

        48
Dornröschen, princess
            are not you too   held
In the crystalline moment of time stopped,
            you lying
So demurely propped,   naked and spelled,
On the couch of stone/
                            The purifying
Of icy fire surrounds you/
                            Beyond it, quelled
Forever, is the what-might-have-been, for you,
            though the unimpelled,
Are the dreamer whose significant dreaming
Still brings,   dream by dream,   the seeming
That will be the world/
                            You lie in the center,
The integration
And the nowhereness of all things,
            as seasons of being turn
            around the winter/
O northern princess,
                            see these apparitions,
How they gather in dreams, our history from the mist,
The meaningless, mysterious images of your dreaming

reason

That you will know

the instant you are really kissed.

4 9

You know what?

What, Amos?

It's Christly strange –

The way we are, I mean. Not like the animals.
I mind one time down to the Grange
Sucking up them venison meatballs
They put on at their annual supper to raise some change,
I seen Yewklid Morrison. Yewk had the mange
And a rumbling gut. He made me think
Of my old Tom after that drink
Of monkeyjuice Luther Parkhurst give him. Hell,
We're all animals deep down,
I reckon. Yet not exactly. I could tell
Yewk was considering, I see him frown,
But I couldn't tell what. And then all those others,
Suddenly they seemed like they came from out of town,
Strangers, though they was my neighbors. Some
was my own brothers.

5 0

Ain't that something? Why, I knowed old Tom
Most as if I was a cat myself,
But not those people. And by God, I'm
People, right? Don't laugh;
To me it's something mighty close to crime.
There ain't none of us real.

Once I come

Down through the old graveyard on Clay Hill
In March in a snowstorm, and I heard a wail
Like all those stones was crying out their names,
And I could hear each one,
Davis and Dodge and Butler, Stearns and James,

And they was all of us, dead bone
Or beating heart, no difference, each a spook,
You, me, or Harpo Marx, and then that stone
You call the woman back there in that brook.

5 1

Your dream:

His name was Hegel, a dear sweet man;
Nay, tho' 'a cou'dst na gabble it straitly, yet he saw
Straightway to the end of the brave Tristan
And the beautiful Iseult,
How they must die, oh, most needfully die, their own
Hands upon it – for sake o' th' higher synthesis. None
Saw it keenlier, none the entire
Realpolitk, how Romance doth aspire
(From those souls bound and dying) to life in the mass,
Freedom in history,
Being in cosmos. Oh, 'a was a darlin' man. Don't ask,
Dear dreamer, for the posterior story
Of life, freedom, and being, or where those bones do lie –
Tristan and Iseult and all. 'Twere mankind's glory,
And thine,
        and in thy dreaming hit mought make thee cry.

5 2

Named she was a Smith, born Smith, but how related
To any Smith on earth? – and she was called Bessie
And papa her beauty wan't very much in her face
Nor body neither she wan't nobody's baby
But she was just the most beautifullest known lady
Cause lord what she was was Woman yes and Grace
And well Sex papa and all them things twice
Over and more in that dark oh that powerful voice

Ain't no high yallah I'm a dee-ep chicken brown

And papa she meant it

For herself and all her people and women
And the human soul yes that's feminine that's musical
And there was a accident lord it was the end of song
Cause Clarksville they shut her out the honky hospital

Oh I'm a young woman
                    singing
            no it won't never end

                    and I ain't done nothing wrong.

            5 3
He reads:
                "That is one of the great tragedies
Of revolutions: you have to suppress man
In order to save him."
                    But o Fidel,
"Suppress" means the camps,
It means "up against the wall," and good Cardenal
Who loves you and your revolution, the equalities,
The courage, the beautiful new nation,
Cardenal saw the camps, saw the oppression,
Cardenal saw the State . . .

                        He reads. He writhes.
He's old almost, he is
Fifty-five, yet still the boy-anarchist. These deaths
Are unbearable. No one is guilty
Enough for that (or everyone is). They say: choose.
But Spirit, he cannot, he can't. Then what shall he
Do?
        Nothing.
                He'll be. And he'll sing the blues.

            5 4
As Rousseau was another, singing.
                        Everywhere man

Is born free, and everywhere
                    he is in chains.
Through history, as if in history's plan,
They rise, they flare like grains
Of meteoric fire, the great romancers, one
Following another, burning, burning.
                                        Men
Must be forced to be free.
                            And passion
In romance must be love in action,
Lust for the ideal . . . oh, murderous . . .

                                    All you great,
All you good and terrible
Straining forever in beauty and man's fate,
You heroes valorous in error,
Why could you not have let love be? And why
Was loving never enough?

                    Sing, Robespierre,
Of how your loves look, trundling past to die.

        5 5
        "Shock? Is that what you're asking? My dear, I was a
country girl, like you, like most of us, you understand?
What didn't we understand – about that! And it's all in the
texts anyway; and yes, there are those who read. You
yourself will learn. Besides,
        It was common knowledge. The seraglio has walls and
the walls have chinks. The real shock – though granted, I
knew it already – was how
        And in what degrees I was expected to conduct myself.
I had not, could not have, altogether anticipated the effect
of that. The bride
        Will smile just so, and just so much, and will bow
        Just here, kneel just there, prostrate herself at just such-
and-such an intimation. Exactness is all. You'll see. It is
called the Formulary of Submissiveness,

Which was without doubt the worst of the instruction,
at least for me. The rest was easy, though I must say
explicit.

Demonstrations with ivory facsimiles, done in
extraordinary detail. When, where, how to touch,

And with what, et cetera. You are smiling? I was told
to crouch

But not to spring, that was the essence. And all in
God's will, of course, and the doing it in His praise. So I did
my best.

Still I confess I never to this day have understood

Why virgins should be the particular gratification of a
lord's lust. Something's peculiar there. You'd think the
contrary, wouldn't you, in spite of the pre-bridal training?
But you are smiling again. You feel differently? You are
thinking perhaps of *your* lust, *our* lust?

Well, as to that, my dear, what is it but service to our
lord, and to such a lord? It is called love; remember that. A
very magnificent lord, no? This is our election. This is what
I was told.

A simulated ecstasy, if practiced to perfection, is better
than actuality. The actual, if unavoidable, is to be strictly
controlled. And so on. Not that I was ever the favorite,

Nor even second or third. And now I am somewhat
old.

Reckon the time yourself if you can: age twelve to
forty-two. Thirty years I've waited for death. And I suppose
'in the nature of things' – oh, patience of impatience! – I may
have another thirty to wait."

  5 6

O.K., Fulke Greville: "None can well behold
With eyes/ But what underneath him lies." You,
Old Yankee progenitor for sure, old
Pragmatist. Yet construe
These that the poem sees, these hot and cold
On the pillow. Such a diversity. The bold
Wet laughter of Grisette, the strained

Nymphomaniacal graduate trained
On pleasure's last least itch, the placid smile
Of true deepgoing rapture,
The cool one coming for friendship's sake, the guile
Or the crude or crazy stare of terror's capture
In ecstasy's last triumph, on the very brink –
Union in love, Fulke Greville? Or union's fracture
As back into Selfhood's mystery all loves sink?

          57
Then rapture is self in itself entranced. And love?
It comes in the understanding that may mean
Not taking, not giving, but just to live –

You see that light on the mountain,
Small in the remoteness of blue snow? Viola
Lives there with her man who is 25 years older
Than she is. And every week
When Viola comes to town, she looks –
Bodily radiance shining in her dark eyes –
At the flatlanders who ask
How she can stand it up there with that old guy.
Do they think Viola wears a mask?

Beyond rapture is freedom, somewhere far above
Or far below, where the self is newly unentranced.
Viola knows. She fucks with an old man.
          Free, living, and without age,
                    and in many ways
                              and at any moment,
                                        they make love.

          58
Your dream:
                    His name is Heraclitus, and he is huge,
Kosmikos, the primeval mentality,
                              his skin

Glowing and changeable and many-hued,
Earthen
      or a pelt of rosmarine
Flaming in aurora.
           And he bends over you as if in
      brooding,
A magnetic cloud,
         and he touches your breast,
               and your
      blood
Rouses in a thickened heat never felt
Until now,
       and his mouth burns on your feet,
Your thighs, your belly, your tongue, your eyes,
            he mounts
Over you and your vagina
Pulses and widens,
        your brain is a tightness, an agony
Of incredulity and eagerness.
          And your raging
Body is broken and shaken in the slow everlasting burst
Of mystery,
      the atomic profusion, the galactic
              fires, winds, oceans,
   and you are
Molten,   undulant,
   conceiving
      the whole idea of the universe.

59

Jays shrieking in the fir clump, a world enraged.
Blue figures hopping in snow – burdened boughs.
What for, Amos?
         Them critturs! Always
Fussing, ain't they? – not like you
Or me.
    Zoön politikon?
         Eyuh. If they ain't got cause

For hollering, they'll make one. But likely they has,
Now, by the sound of it.
                              Three bounds
In deep snow and the cat pauses, looking around
And up, forepaw in a curl and her eyes
Triangular with indignation.
The jays dive-bomb her, the shrieking intensifies,
She cowers.
                    See? All that hell-raising
For a yaller kitty. And she wan't jay-hunting. Twelve
Below and she's hungry, just trying for a mouse-nest.
Them jays, they ought to be ashamed of theirself.

                    6 o

He goes out with his chainsaw into the cold bright
Winter morning, into the forest. The cabin
Needs fuel, it always needs fuel. The night
Has dropped snow, eleven
Inches gauged on the brown ash, a sagging weight
On his snowshoes. And he sings,
                              My gal's gotta light
Like a lighthouse out to sea.
                         And oh,
You loves, say,
                    do you feel him bestow
Loving on you, which is a valuing? It is your beauty
Given to you in his seeing,
Your intelligence in his thought, so that truly
You become, you are becoming, in his being,
As he in yours. For loving is how you create
Each other, all of you, bestowing and believing
Together.
                    Well, my gal's gotta light like a light-

                    6 1

House out to sea.
                    And he has dropped a dead gray birch

In the snow and is limbing it when his left snowshoe
Slips. Snarling, the saw leaps; he lurches;
The chain snags his bootlace –
And the motor stalls. Gasp. He looks at his unsevered
Foot in astonishment. Alone, completely, in the forest.

(So many tone-rows. Spirit, will
They ever come together?)

                              You call,
One by one, lovers, through the distances: He's alive!
Alive!
        He yanks the lanyard
And begins bucking the birch for his Glenwood stove.
Alive. Somehow it is important,
Not because he matters, himself there like a tree
Among other trees, but because you have accorded it.

And ever' time she smile she shine her light on me.

        6 2
Your dream:
                His name was Hermes, and he was all to all,
The thief loved by peasants, who thus made him their boundary
Keeper and took him friendlily for their god
Of place and property;
Yet he was a great musician. He rejected the old
Conservatory music and sang the blues in a mode
Anyone could respond to. So they wanted him
Close by them always; he was psychopompos
Conducting their dead souls to hell, and he was herm,
Their phallus in the garden,
Guardian of the bed.
               He is guardian of your dream,
Dear sleeper,
            uniter of commerce and art,
Possession and beauty. His cleverness permits your world,

For he is your holy hermetic hoodlum, your secret.
Yet he told it all to Dionysus, your dreadful child.

63

Your dream:

His name was Husband, his title Herr,
Noblest denomination, since he came from God
In the olden tongue. So he was tiller of your
Sweet soil, as of your close abode
Defender, and his rod was magical. Given to war
It was the onthrusting blade, or in your fire
The gentle stoker. And at times he rode a horse,
Going before you, and at times a hearse,
Leading the way to heaven.

But first and always
He was Herr Husband,
Householder, Handyman to all your joys,
And if he stumbled or looked askance
You had only to think your clever sexual thought
That brought him to his parfit gentillesse again,
Your knightly teacher whom none but you had taught.

64

The full of the moon. In pine woods a snowlight
Shines under the trees everywhere and is shadowless.
It were as if an earthlight, bright
Only by day's absence,
Arose, mysteriously radiant, in the night –
"But reflection, it is all reflection." High and white,
The moon looks down on her sister,
Who gazes back, askance, eastward,
Alone in the water. This is a spectral instance,
Light as it is in dreaming,
Its twice angled remoteness a transcendence
Or an alluding sourcelessness, a seeming,
Which only mythological sisters may embody

In this world. Cycle and stasis. Gleaming
And obscure. These two, together and solitary.

6 5

Odds & ends:
                    Enosburg Falls & Geof's cabin,
The lamplight, a fir bough scratching the eaves,
Snow kicking the windows. Geof croons
To his Mexican jumping bean,
"Hey friend, little worm, come out – don't you long
To come out?" Answer: "He's probably wondering
Why in God's name you don't come in."
And Janet laughed & laughed, and everyone
Had another slug of Geof's reefer.
                                        Postscriptum
In medias . . .
                    And meanwhile
Margery weeps. The first year, aphasic, bedridden,
Paralyzed – still her courage held;
But now the second. "She cries a lot." Hey friend,
Little Spirit,

                have you got any power?

                                        Delirium,
This talk of art & love, the odds & the ends!

6 6

He remembers:
                    There was this big house they called the Hatch,
Or sometimes the Laughing Academy, which had barred grilles
On its windows, for every door a latch
And an appropriate lock called Yale
That was big and brassy with a key in someone else's possession,
And inside there he suffered interrogation, torture
When they wired his head to voltage and shocked him
Deep into the abyss, so that when he woke

He couldn't remember who he had been, and they did it
Again and again, and he sighed,
"Why? What have I done?" and usually they evaded
The question, but sometimes they said,
"Nothing, son, nothing at all – you're just unlucky,"
And he stood by the window in a dirty draft of cold,
Looking out, and he saw benches and sidewalks

67

Rise up and proclaim themselves, and his skin
Crawled on his body, a tear strolled down his nose,
And months later they said again,
"You're jinxed, son, you'll always
Be this way," and he saw his life sink down
In a melted gray heaving mass like a broken brain,
The chairs ignored him, the calendar
On the wall masturbated shamelessly, relentlessly,
Until years later they said, "O.K., you can go now,
Everything has been done,"
And he stepped to the door, but then he did not know how,
And he turned as if he had lost someone,
And they threw him out, and "Why?" he still whispered,
    "Why?"
Knowing no answer would come to him under the sun
Or anywhere else, whether he should live or die.

68

Your dream:
        His name was Hendryk Hudson. And oh, the glory!
Sailing so splendidly up that lordly river,
White canvas arching!
            Could any story
From the time before forever
Ever be more entrancing?
           Yes, that was very
Nearly what it was, sunlight so merry

On the wavelets, white clouds mirroring
Those brave sails.
                    Such a northfaring!
And such a land, this land, the *new found land*,
        hills
Greening on every side,
Appearing all as if from beyond time,
                                    and all
For you, dear sleeping princess.

                        Hide,
O Spirit – can you? – her dream from the blood those shores
Will come to. Can you?

                    How beautiful! What pride –
The little *Half Moon*, sailing her *tour-de-force!*

        6 9
Shall he then finally "put away childish things,"
Cunts, cocks, and similar ornaments, being
Grown old? So crude, so sudden. He sings
The blues in a broken singing
Now, impotent, croaking the anesthetic sting
Of loneliness. Shall he compose
        the obligatory abjuring,
Greville's Fare-thee-well to desiring,
Donne's Good-bye, sweet world,
        so soon, so abruptly?

                    Waking
At dawn, drawn curtains edged with light, finding
This silken blood-purse clinging,
Body so loved, woman in all her glistening,
Begging his entrance, and more worth entering
Than the caves of childhood, he, hot with the breath
Of essential animation, living and making,
Cannot.

Your touch, dear sorceress.

                    Damn it, is that your best?

7 0

Bleakness in the town.

                Each house wears a grimace
Under the wind, cold and phlegmatic. Along the streets
Lie clots of old blood that are really ice.
And at Dunkin' Donuts, across
The loop of the counter, sit two young women, pristine,
Beautiful – one with her hair cropped, her face
Clear as the Cupbearer's, three rings
Of Indian silver on her fingers
That are deft with cigarettes and matches; the other
Fuller, softer, with reddening
On her nails, her hair flowing and dark. They are
So deeply in love. "Bless you, children,"
He says to the steam in his coffee. "May my weakness
Somehow still swell in your ardors a little, unbidden."
Can such transmittance be?

                  Out to the bleakness.

7 1

His body, caught there in the mirror, lean
With an old man's hunger, though he turns quickly –
Not quickly enough – away. He has seen
Taut sinews, muscles thickly
Knotted with useless decades of strength, his skin
Creased and flaccid. This is an apparition
Out of an old book, an anatomy
Lesson, he cannot be that,
He is still the young swollen tree forever
And no gnarled bough
On an old oak rotting.

           Spirit, deliver
Him to the true knowledge of death. He knew

It was easy. Now teach him arduousness,
How it comes slowly, how gradually, and how
An old oak declines, twig by twig, in the forest.

7 2

Your dream:
                His name was Hitler and he lived over
The yelping forest where wolves run bearing the bones
Of Tristan back and forth forever.
In a castle, in firelit rooms,
His shadow passes, enigma of the gothic tower
Become the home of horror. See there, a sword
Hopping on a hare's foot, or a disembodied
Arm that floats stiff in a bloodied
Sleeve, or maybe a boot slopping with hot liquid
That you know is not what it seems;
And there, that indeflatable phallus disguised in a hood
With one hole for the hangman's eye. Screams
You cannot hear issue from mouths you cannot mistake
In each stone of the walls. So you make your dreams
Of Hitler, you also screaming, knowing you cannot wake.

7 3

"They tossed my baby like a cat in the air
And caught him on a lance-tip, and he slid back,
Entrails popping, face gone black. 'Here,'
I gasped, bending my neck,
'Here, now here!' flinging apart my hair,
Gesturing for the blade; but they only sneered
And threw me down in the dirt and forced me,
Seven of them, with the murdering all around me,
Stench and blood and shrieking. Then they left me,
I don't know why. I begged
For the sword.
                Now more than a year after
I have this pale-eyed, wolf-pelted, thick-legged
Child. Revenge! Yet, O Ormuzd, when I get out

My knife I still see my other one, still pegged
On the lance-shaft, and I cannot.

                              Why! Why can I not?"

        7 4
Your dream:
                    Her name was Hestia, sister of God
And goddess of the hearth, a brown woman and ageless,
But known to be very, very old
And very silent. She blessed
Any house that had become a home, and so guarded
Its sanctity, yet she could dwell in the dark
Cinders as well as the glowing, and she
Was silent. Somehow this made her free
In spite of her duties. She could be felt in an instant
If the house went wrong,
If love there were not voluntary, or if wanting
Drove away giving. Silence was her song.
It meant freedom in loving. Princess, you would invoke
Hestia for your dream, but she gave you a long
Cold silent look. And, princess, you almost woke.

        7 5
Why is the face in the water a woman? Because
Rita made it? Because she said it? But it could
Be a man, indistinct there, that gaze
Across eternity. Would
Other women see a man in the water, a case
Of anima/animus? No, they all always
Know that the water-person is a woman,
Just as the poem knows, the poem
Which is both. Then is it convention, the cultural
Input: Naiad, Ophelia?
Partly perhaps. But more it's a question of structural
Consciousness. For the image is basal,
From before the beginning of all imagining,
The *a priori* of human feeling, ineffaceable

For good or for ill,
     and as such it is,   it must be,   feminine.

7 6

Making love in the cabin, not to himself
This time, a visitor has come to him, has come
With him. Then, lying there, he recalls
That for a long (eternal?) moment
His being and hers were indistinguishable,
So intermingled that he could not tell
Which was man, which woman. Is that
What Plato meant by the reunited
Soul? Or only his sex-whelmed mind defecting?
Neither hypothesis
Appeals to him. He knows his feminine aspect,
Always his, deeply and dearly his.
He wonders: necessarily so are we all
And why is it hidden? Without this synthesis
How could we be, alone or together, whole?

7 7

It was Catlett driving, de Paris blowing strong,
And James P., the incomparable – he could play
Anything. But that day all along
Had been Ben Webster's, as he made that old song
Leap out of itself in greatness, never to belong
To anyone else. Oh, far and wide
The spit sprayed out on either side
Of his number seven reed to create that breathy
Tone, those growls, those flutters,
Which are all most people hear in their deafness;
But it was music, music. What matters
Was oneness, the abstract made personal in a tone.
You in your transcending freedom, never another's
Ever again,
       Ben Webster,   after you've gone.

78

He thinks of classical women:

                          Helen, Julia,

Thaïs, Amarintha . . .

                    Amarintha? He smiles,

In disdain, in love. It was mythopoeia,

The convention that beguiles

Itself and its successors in a pure euphoria

Of idealization. Julia had no wart? Or

Cynthia no straggling yellow tooth?

Then they were mere conceptions, youth

Feminized, sexual but eternal, held

In the long access of rhyme

That you, dear dreamer, are inventing,

                              romance unwilled

And unrelenting.

                  And yet that time,

He thinks, was actual; they lived, unknown women,

Flawed and misnamed, their soft rank bodies prime

For idealization. Convention is also human.

79

Near Addison now.

                See that place over there

With the busted gable?

                Yes, Amos.

                    Terrible

Ain't it? All tumbledown. That's where

Dorothy lives, old Doll.

I knowed her once. By the sweet Jesus she were

The prettiest thing you ever seen. I courted her,

Courted her crazy, hot like I was –

Me and a parcel of other hornies –

But Doll couldn't never settle. Or wouldn't.

Screwed whatever come around,

Thirteen kids and not one father amongst them,

Not as would take her off the town.

She'd be screwing yet if she could. Maybe she does,
Though I hear she hefts to nigh two-fifty pound.
Mostly she hooks rugs. You know that kind they call
*   "The Blowing Rose"?*

8 0

Your dream:
                    Its name apparently is Honeywell,
But what is it? A tree of thorns, a bush, a vine
Tangled with many others, a wall
Encircling you, entwined
Twig to twig, thorn to thorn, like fire?
                                        Hell
Hath such fires, burning and consuming, themselves
Never consumed.
                    Out of the circle
Come voices corporate and low:
                            "Oh darling,
Thank you, thank you, we are eternally yours. Only
Stay as you are and we'll burn,
We'll consume forever, and we promise there'll be hotels
On Boardwalk and Park, and champagne, furs,
Weekends in Spain, anything you want,
                                    you won't be forsaken,
But we'll love and protect you as long as the world is ours,
As long as we burn, as long as you never waken."

8 1

In France, through archways, the archaic stonework
So adorned by time, he wandered the Basse-Ardèche –
Labeaume, Burzet, Roche-Colombe, Balazuc,
Towns lichened in ancientness,
Their crumbled châteaux, walls that a *trobador* took
With a song, blood-dark still where the Languedoc
Shed fierce heretical love. He wandered.
Beauty is pain plus time. Why then
Does he stay so cold? It's true, he could be at home,

And he thought of his own north,
Frozen roads, patchwork villages. He knew
The differences, of course – colors, textures of earth,
Viticulture against dairying – and also the similarities,
Les pauvres de tous côtés et le désespoir,
He knew all right; but his heart was a cavity

82

Voided by too many hopes betrayed, too many
Failures. All is irrelation. What power
Could make unity? Has love any
Left in its broken tower?
What draws these themes together? Not ceremony,
That lost vantage; not belief. "The universe has only
The unity possessed by any heap."
Fact! A good fact, good to keep
(His William James) in the pocket of his mind
For a talisman. At least
It's a kind of unity, this heap, this undesigned
Collection – snow-laden spruce
And sunburnt ilex. Then there's another. Alone,
Always alone, he knew the body of loneliness,
Stone, universal stone, and the face in the stone.

83

La colline du mystère. Solitary here. The stone,
The old crown, is exposed, fissured, worn
By time's aimlessness, the wind and rain;
Crumbled; inscrutable; strewn;
Pieces porous and bleached, thousands, like bone.
Here on the height, alone, stands the great dolmen,
Three slabs set upright and another,
The table, a massive stone, laid over.
Une présence absolue. Inexorable, majestic,
There! And what made those
Shadowy absences, those drifted generations, wrest
And drag and raise such stones? Who knows –

Except that it was belief. It is always belief.
And forgotten. Lost. The dolmen is silent. It glows
Almost, thunderous almost, in its sanctity of grief.

8 4

No love without hurt? No lovesong without distortion?
Maybe the dolmen-makers, whose art was their dinner,
Cutlets on the cave wall, and whose fashion
Of coupling was no doubt similar,
Knew more about it than we do and were right to lavish
Their loving on the dead. Is love from the grave,
Love's imagery raked from that nostalgia,
That bitterness?
                              Think of the Sangraal
And the unicorn, dear sleeper, your dream's burden,
Essential love and death.
Your couch, brocaded like veined stone, might be the
            dolmen.
But another way must come, princess,
We must love humanly, no debasement. We must sing
Our passion, as ineluctable as breath,
Without distortion, yet still this wondrous thing.

8 5

Then here was where it began, dear sleeping princess,
This stony land with its stony great *châteaux*,
Your dream's origin and focus,
The sweet song that somehow rose
As from the stone itself, *rime claire et douce,*
To sing old *joi, valor, mesura* – oh, loveliness
Beyond all preconceiving. This,
This land of *òc,* is where your kiss
Awaits you . . .
                              land of blood, of class, of hunger.
For here a song could nearly
Make nature from the world's pain, sex from anger,
A woman from death.

But knowingly, drearily
Now we hear – so far, so near – the *trobador*
Sing, *Òc, Dieu d'amor* – wistfully, wearily –
Quora me donas jòi, quora me'n ven dolor.

86

Your dream:
His name was Harlequin. He wore the mask
That hides identity, which in one sense made him false.
Or in another universal, and yes, you longed to ask;
Yet you only waltz'd and waltz'd,
Tango'd, lindy'd, hustl'd, sipped from his flask
And fled with him down dim cellarways
as down the years
to the farthest, darkest cask –
Ah, was it Venice, Vienna? No matter,
Dresden will do as well. The clatter
Of years falling, decades, was like music. *O carnevale!*
Granted, his aspect was inhuman,
But why not? Who better than he who was holy
(Or might be) could keep you, dreaming woman,
Safe in your mythical cities?
And if in his mask you glimpsed
his eyes
And were saddened,
that also seemed expected,
a part of the common
Ceremony,
like a grief-rite or the children's promised surprise.

87

He decided to live. Alone. One room. Quaking.
Word by word he forced his poems on his rigid
Tongue. Outside, the universe smirked,
Massive, mindless, the official
Existence taunting him, haunting him, seeking

To brush him away, crush him, annihilate him, make
A no-person. And inside, meanwhile,
Simpering oblivion smiled
From every darkness, corner of room or of mind,
Beckoning as if
She could redeem, merely by her own kind
Of kindness, a murdering touch or a kiss,
His sick penis. Should he acquiesce? Very often
His longing, his simple undifferentiated wistfulness,
Almost convinced him. Yet he was anarchist, lover,

8 8

And he stood at his window and shook his fist at a cloud.
It didn't help much. It helped a little. Denial
Became, he saw, the one defense allowed
In this one-room, one-person trial
That went on for years. Well, he prayed to Ungod,
Loved, and declined to be insane. He stood
At his window for hours, by night and by noon,
Watching the bellylaughing moon,
The derisive trees, the mocking street, the cars
Singing their death-joy, the students
Walking from school and already fading, pears
Tainted on the tree. Terrified, he went
Over his terrified lines, no by no. If one shred
Of consciousness remained, one infinitesimal root
Of freedom, he swore he would save it. And he did.

8 9

The springtime so impetuous. Already pink blossoms
Are drifting down, a flurry in the peach grove
At the high end of the *vallon*. Sometimes
They become less pink than mauve,
Less mauve than deep rose, when clouds hide the sunshine
And the mountains darken. Then again they are gossamer
Weaving in brightness, falling, billowing,
Wavering. The old brown woman below

At her goat-tending looks up to see them and to see
The mysterious wind spun
From mountain stone that takes them, whirls them free
And up, up, in a vortex. With them
Her eyes too move upward. For always there is a falling
And a rising within, this beautiful helical rhythm,
And always, it seems, a vision calling and calling.

90

"My mother did it. She had to, she said. She took
Ten yards of binding cloth and wrapped my toes
Backward underneath like a broken book.
Then came the embroidered shoes,
Smaller and smaller for two years, and so I forsook
My childhood, which was my only life. Now look –
You see a Chinese lady, sixteen,
Stylish and sexy and properly constrained
For her bridegroom, who has never seen my feet
And never will, just my pretty
Three-inch shoes. Inside are pain and heat
Perpetual. They never stop. Well, I totter
In this garden, snipping carnations. Is there another
System, do you think, where girls run and a daughter
Smiles? You smile. Yes, in a year I shall be a mother."

91

Came in upon him once how he might find
A freedom neither in woman nor in art.
Faith, he thought. Is it always blind?
Then the Saltmaker's part
In India he took, and of his chosen kind
At home the Dreamer's, walking through Georgia. Mind
Gave him to see them clearly, not
Ideas alone but anguish caught
In their living brains, a rational belief;
From which he saw as well
(For him afresh) how madness or any life

Lived in devotion is therefore whole,
Self-committed and therefore free, nor less
For its passivity what one could call
Powerful still in mankind's saintliness.

9 2
Your dream:
                    His name was Heathcliff, and he was clearly
The invention of a subsidiary dreamer,
Yet how? Was he gross a little, obscurely
Not of the true demeanor,
Overdrawn? What fault was there? You loved him fairly
And could no less, since no one could say he really
Had broken the pattern. It is confusing.
His eyes are a deep darkness, losing
The pure reflection of yourself you cherished,
Which makes you love more intensely,
Suspecting your true intensity has perished.
This dream is awkward.
                              Lovely princess,
Rose, are you weary now? Do you merely laugh
At all these dreaming dreams, you who are thinking
How your own great dream has departed from itself?

9 3
Your dream:
                    At first its name is Heliopolis,
Beyond the Land of Goshen, where ruins have spread
Since before anyone's memory, city
Of the red sun, blasted,
Hyssop and mandrake growing in jagged fissures
And scarabs clicking in the heat. It is the center
Of known earth, ruined for all
History; it is the mouth of hell
Where hot light pours down and vanishes. So
In your dream you change its name
To Hiroshima, the city where stone-edges glow

And shadows burn in the unimaginable time
Of half-life, city of the man-made sun. Your breath
Burns in your throat. This is the most extreme
Moment of dreaming. You sleep and are close to death.

94

The poem moves.
                 After the fierce intention,
The exalting, reaching and thrusting through lust,
Through densities of image, to explode transcendence
From a broken language, to touch
Everyone's wordlessness, to crush what was meant
Till it dances clear of language like forestfire bent
And flaring in the wind –

                  Snow dances
Like fire sometimes, windblown.
                      Jesus,
Watch it! They're off the road.
                  The pickup whines
And skids in a flying drift
Of snow, wild night in the headlights. Someone
Helpless there, tentatively lifting
Her hands – down jacket, platinum hair, suede pants.
Back up then, turn, hook on the chain, shift
To low range, second gear, ease the clutch – wince

95

As the broken front differential pops and jumps –
But out she slips, the Mercedes with Connecticut plates,
Dragging packed snow. At once
One face goes flat,
A mask now, and a thin-gloved hand plunges,
Comes out with a twenty, an offering, a vengeance,
Insisting, commanding.
               The wind screams.
                  Unhook

The chain, belly-down in snow. Then:
>   *Look,*
Lady . . .
>   *Look, it ain't fitten. This is nothing*
We do for the money. Take
It somewhere else.
>   And the twenty flutters,
Gasping like a fish.

>   Amos, what makes them think
They can buy us?
>   *They done it – stone by stone,*
Tree by tree, running brook by brook.
Hell, you and me is just something else to own.

96

It's awful, Amos.
>   *Well, of course you could say*
It starts mostly with a kind of loving. They wouldn't
Come here if they didn't like it. Why,
You and me our own selves
Don't hardly see it; don't hardly see the sky,
Nor those hills or woods or pastures. We got our eye
Always looking down in a milk pail
Or a sap bucket or up the hole
Of one goddamn animal or another to see
What ails her. We been here
Too long, wearing our butts down. But those city
People, downcountry millionaires,
They see, you bet your ass they see, our farms,
Our hills and fields, all those shapes and colors
Always changing; well, by the sweet Jesus it warms

97

Our own hearts too like, seems's-zo, whenever
We stop to look – it's only the best goddamn place
In the world. And them, those billionaires –

Couldn't tell a trace
From a bellyband, but they can see what's here
All laid out for them, see it some ways clearer
Than us, damn their hides, so they "falls
In love with it" – you know their flashy
Way of talking. And what do those trillionaires do
When they fall in love with something,
Almost anything? They buy it, that's what. So
Maybe it ain't just right to blame them.
They wants it and they got the power to get it,
So they gets it. You and me might do the same.
Only then the poor bastards come to feeling guilty,

98

Maybe because they're so damn frigging rich,
Or maybe for shoving some farmer off his land
Or the townfolk out of their housen, them which
Has come down hand to hand
For generations. So they get in a twitch
All proud and feisty-like, and it makes them itch
To buy more, and buy and buy and buy
Till they own most everything. That's why
They think they own the people too, and by God
They do, at least a good cross
Section of us. Hell, you stick a big enough wad
Of that green stuff under the nose
Of a Vermonter and he'll grab. You bet he'll grab,
Same as anyone else. And yet –

                            some of us
Won't. A few. Our own kind of pride, or crabbiness,

99

Or independence, call it what you blame well like.
There's some as might just call it a kind of loving,
But the other kind, the kind that makes
You give and go on giving,
Just like that, and if you get something back

You're grateful, but you don't ever ask, you don't ever take,
You don't ever own. That's the difference.
Some of us knows it, or senses it,
Us old north country uglies that can love a barn
Or a cow or a woman. You build
Fences to keep the animals out of the corn,
Not for a property line. A field
Is a speck of creation, just like –

                                Ho, back down,
Amos, you're preaching now. Men here have killed
For a half-acre, and many a time. You know it.

                                                No one

                I O O

Better, goddamn it. Why, whenever I see folks
I growed up with get so narrow-like I want
To resign, all those would-be bankers
Fighting over a misdrawn
Deed, which ain't the whole of it neither. Just think
How many of these so-called developers, these speculators,
Was home-raised country boys. We ain't
No better than we should be. But there wan't
No surveyors till the rich folk came. Them old deeds
Was drawn for a convenience
Mostly, and some of us knowed it. Likely we be
Gone now. But by God, a field is
A speck of creation, same as you or me,
So how can you own it? Tilling it is the yield.
You get because you give

                                if the giving's free.

                I O I

Some don't get much, Amos.

                                Some, hell! Most
Is what you mean. Look at all these boneyards around here
Cram-full of them that give up the ghost
From nothing but despair,

You can damn near hear them sighing. They lost, lost
Till they couldn't lose no more, and they wouldn't cost
The state for welfare. So they lay down,
Took sick, and died – that's how it's done.
Simple. What I was talking about is not
A program, like those extension guys
With their technology; it's a feeling or a thought
Or both maybe, I don't know. Some ways
It don't work so good, like nature herself, like
A hen partridge setting six weeks on a clutch of eggs
Ain't even fertile. But look there now.

The truck

1 0 2

Slows. A bent figure in the dark, thickly clothed,
An ash staff in one mitten, flashlight in the other,
Slow-stepping from house to barn.

Something's

Making that guy a bother
On a stormy night. A calving, likely. What's it worth?
Salt, coffee, a pack or two of Day's Work,
And not a hell of a sight more,
That's what he gets. Just one damn chore
After another. And yet look, that henhouse out beyond,
The woodshed and the shop,
The snowy scarecrow where the garden is, that pond
On the lower side, and over the slope
I bet you'll find an orchard keeping warm.
That light is a woman making coffee, up
And ready, case she's needed out to the barn,

1 0 3

Which ain't much barn at that, maybe twenty head.
Yet they're Jerseys – can't you almost tell? –
Or even Ayrshires, sorrel red
And sweet and trained to the bell,
None of those ugly stupid Holsteins bred

With udders so big they can't hardly walk. It's dead,
Some say, all gone, finished, sunk.
Ten years sober or four years drunk
Is what I'd give this farmer. But what he gets
Is what he's got, a place,
Not just a farm but a place: sunrises and sunsets
And no damn zillionaires. And then a space
In the boneyard. Gone. Goddamn it, I feel old –
Not because I am, but the land is going, the base.
Aw, it ain't but ten below, but God it's cold.

104

Your dream is Hamlet again:

                                        Is not he
Recurrent in all these appearances, the one
Prince of the North who took from sea
And solitude and stone
The thought that someone somewhere might be free?
In pain now he looks down, thinking "for me,"
Down to Ophelia in her weedy stream

Where you gaze back. You know your dream
Is his sanity and his insanity. You know
He cannot see your tears,
The endless colorless weeping into the flow
Of time, nor can he read your fears
Concerning the inevitability of act five
When you cry love! and no dead actor hears,

O princess,
                        drowned in dreaming, asleep, alive.

105

In the mind's house of heaven the great night never
Ends.
        All the brothers are there: Berigan, Bechet,
Russell, Hawkins, Dickenson, Hodges,

And Mary Lou and Lady Day
And so many others.
                        And oh they play, they
      jam forever,
Shades of strange souls nevertheless caught together
In eternity and the blues.
                        No need
To cut anyone any more, no fatigue
From the straights out front or the repetitive changes,
But only expressiveness, warmth,
Each invention a purity, new without strangeness
In that session.
                        Always they strained on earth
For this thing, skin and soul to merge, to disappear
In howling sound.
                        God, but it would be worth
Dying, if it could be done,
      to be there with them and to hear,   to *hear*.

        1 0 6
Nine, he thinks, and every one a failure.
Is it accident only, the actual number,
The same as the primeval female
Faces, the nine in one?
What does that mean? And how can freedom prevail
When every lover's gift is a day in hell?
Is this finally what the face in the water
Is saying, that everyone is caught
In the terrible twist at the pit of consciousness? One
Never escapes, never.
And the sweet anarchist dream of love is gone?
What can he do, culprit forever,
But remove himself, destroy his insanity? And the mill
Of the species, grinding new culprits, new lovers,
What can it do but vanish?
                        Well, he thinks, it will.

107

Your dream:

        His name was unheard of, very strange,
As he himself, moving in your mind's shadows,
Gliding there in perpetual change
Like a shape on starlit meadows
In a far deserted land, was a kind of outrage
And a very deep disturbance, a danger
You had not known. He whispered, "Lady,
Will you see me, see my body
Altering in starlight, one and one and one?"
And you shuddered. Why
Was this important? What had this outrage done
To you, your world, your dream? A cry
Of anger stirred you, and then a cry of fright,
And then a broken, wistful, subsiding sigh.
You knew. You whispered back, "Hermaphrodite."

108

Your dream:

        Its peculiar name is Hydrogen Bomb,
Meaningless and menacing like the Minotaur
To which young couples once had come
Through their labyrinthine hour
Of passionate initiation, as to the calm
Pitiless unknown of fate. The horn of the ram
Sounds once, twice at the awful door
Of innermost darkness, and more
Cannot be said, cannot be dreamt, for this
Is the ultra-future to which
No experience leads. It is the abyss.
All is vague. Yet was not each
Dream always precisely made for this power
At the heart of darkness, this violence, this beast
Of non-existence hulking beyond your horror?

109

He thinks in wonder how love was all that was
At the beginning/
                    The little human creature
In its blood-cave knew nothing else,
But only love, its nurture,
Its garment, its pulsing name, its pain and ease,
Its world. Then came/

                    the emerging, the cold. Cause
Separated at once from effect,
A thing to be observed. Act
Was all/
             and love like dropped mercury scattered
In its parts, wandering, mirroring,
Called by such names as fear, greed, altruism, hatred,
The shattered self. World was a sorrowing,
Many voices, always cold . . . /

                         Oh, take them then,
These strangely precious fragments, involve them,
        thou spirit-bearing
Word,
        in their old oneness,
                         that they may be love again.

110

He was a soldier, he was a madman, he was a hermit,
Always in deprivation, always in love.
The cast-out seraph within him yearns
For the unattainable, to give,
To give and give: to the wounded, imprisoned, poor,
And ever to women, the captive people. What for?
He asked and asked. No death delayed,
Not one lover was left undismayed
In her ego torture. Love solves nothing. He matured
In despondency, the old deep
Melancholia. But again what for?

                                    The abhorred
Stars in their slow explosion creep
Through the sky, mindless, and the mindless moon
Is a loveliness that mocks him.
                                    Mind is sleep,
Dream, evolutionary error,
                                    bound for extinction soon.

        I I I
He used to think his escape was in lucidity
And refusal and rebellion. But against that?
To see now is to see futility.
The stars creep. What
Is human "authenticity" then but a nullity
Striving to create a value and getting beauty
Instead, dripping with blood. Will
Is the will to exploit. But still
In his depression deepening toward paralysis
He has one more task.
Driven in blindness, driven as the stars in their orbits,
Knowing the outcome will be grotesque,
A pain beyond bearing, and with nothing left to prove,
He must go to the princess. With nothing left to ask,
He must go,
        the prince who is human, driven, and filled with love.

        I I 2
Your dream:
                The letters H I V appear
As if in blood on the wall of consciousness
And a voice comes out of the air,
Your own voice, saying, "Yes,
Human immunodeficiency virus, my dear,
For you in the heart of love."

                        So near,
The breakdown of nature? Was

Sexual order from which rose
Everything you know or make or see
So insubstantial, fallen
Like a house of cards now, jumbled, crazy,
Useless? The wind still blows, the sullen
Sea still beats. You had only to think
A crack in reality, and there it is, appalling –
You and everyone standing there on the brink.

1 1 3
Any fire will do – you who are sleeping
In "a nest of flames," Dornröschen, Brunnhilde,
In the red, red thorns, in petals fleeting –
Any burning city . . .

A fire-storm occurs when the degrees of heat
Reach 1100 Fahrenheit. Flame spreads in sheets,
A huge wind rises, soon the oxygen
Is exhausted.
                    Three attacks: Mosquitoes,
Lancasters, Fortresses, with long-ranging Mustangs
To strafe the crowds.
                    Next day
A leopard from the zoo sprawled in a plane tree
With two naked women below
In the charred boughs. Everywhere soldiers tried
To cremate heaped bodies with flame-throwers. Now
The smell thickens, ashes still fall, Dresden has died.

1 1 4
People burned, came apart, suffocated, melted.
They drowned in the Elbe trying to flee the flames.
The Zwinger was rubbled, the gardens, the Altstadt
Everywhere crazed, that porcelain
City,
        "Florence of the North,"
                            stone which exulted

For beauty, flesh for romance, all split, all spilt.

Death,
        you can be kind. You kiss
Lovers in their blissfulness. Is this
Your doing?

           Where little flames still flicker
Like rings of thorn, a crazy
Man in a smoldering coat, bloody, blistered,
Wanders and mumbles, utterly crazy,
Poking the darkness, the ashes, stumbling, rebuking
The corpses of children, crazy, crazy, crazy,
Wandering, crying, laughing, cursing, looking.

     1 1 5
In wavering shadow and silted with soot, her face
Seems as if almost dreaming, as if under water,
Where she lies in one more ruined place
In this history of the Slaughter
Of the Innocents. How beautiful. The disgrace
Of love's civility riven like the lace
From her own breast, of death and pain
And lamentation and blood, the stain
Contaminating all the bright world she has made
Seem not to touch her.
He gazes down at her, insane, afraid,
For this will be the end. Never
Will our world lie again in her dream's keeping.
He bends to her, the real and loving other.
She wakes,
       sees,
          screams.
             She begins her weeping.

116

Destinies, destinations: In Morrisville
Where the snow, grimed with salt-slush, is roof-high,
Two fat women, maybe nineteen
Or twenty, issue sidewise
From Tomlinson's Deli, eating without smiles
Something from the sacks clutched to their snowmobile
Jackets. Their breath is steam. They climb
Into an object of rust, which has five
Kids in the back with a black and white shepherd dog,
And one sack passes rearward.
Then this thing in its thingness, this '67 Pontiac
Stationwagon, farts. Black gore
Sags from its underside. Roaring with anger,
It spins and slews, and they wobble away, gone –
One wonders where.
                    Why up over the Ben Franklin

117

Store, more'n likely, in one of those tenements.
Notice them childern? They'll eat the mice
Out of the mousetraps when that there candy
Gives out, of course unless
Their old man poaches them a half of venison
And sneaks it up some morning about 4:00 A.M.

Above Eden Mills a barn flattened,
Splayed and shattered under the weight
Of snow.
                    It were a good-looking hip-roof barn,
Long and narrow, when I passed
This way last summer.
                              It's another farm
Gone – snow four feet deep around the house,
"For Sale" on a porch column with the agent's name
In big letters:
                    FRANCIS COLE.

Good man, Francis.
Hates what's been happening round here, same

1 1 8

As you or I, but at least he fights hard to get
A right price for the victims. They trust old
Francis.

       Then in Lowell, the woodland cut
Over and over until all
That's left are thousands of red maple suckers and bent
Gray birches crowding a little trailer with a huge tent
Of snow covering one side.
An old woman trudges with an armload
Of softwood slabs toward the door with its garland
Of Christmas bulbs, a naked
Festoon. But the woods are gone.

            And the Opera
In Derby Line is gone. The theater,
Gone. The music, gone.
          Where? Where?

               Maybe

Where I'm going.
      You?
        Me. You yourself said it,
I'm nowhere. Right?
        Amos, you're in history.

1 1 9

Hah! Not what's wrote down, I reckon. I'm leaving
Now.
      Leaving? You don't want to see the end?
                I seen it
Already, and besides I ain't even
Got enough Yankee meanness

Left for talking about what's happened. And grieving –
What's the use of it? I'll get off here. You needn't
Stop. So long. I'll see you later.

So long, Amos.
    Later?
       Stay here,
Amos, for God's sake! DON'T GO NOW!

          Nowhere . . .
And you, all of you,
Are you gone? Where is the richness of the manure
That used to steam on the snow? Some chemical
Rots the air. Are you gone? Is the land given
Forever to these mechanical monsters risen from Hell?
Look at them, the clones, smiling like Richard Nixon.

   I 2 0
Spirit
   whatever you are wherever
        Amos
Who is nowhere has been one of your emissaries
And a better than many, whence may his loss
Be told among the stories
Of the mythic people, like all those others, those
Who have lived for you, the insane prince, the inconsolable
Princess now at last in their song
Of injured bodies touching, tongue
To tongue, sorrow to sorrow, lust to lust,
A surmounting, a broken flower
In the ashes of their burnt garden, or in the dust
Of history, and then all who in their hour
Have spoken for you here, the brief attendance
Of voices and dreams.
     Spirit
      whatever
      now in your own power

Speak,

       as the poem rises toward you in your resplendence.

     1 2 1

The border is what creates illegal aliens,
Dividing what one knows from what one knows,
This called an "imaginary line,"
Not even drawn on the snow,
With a huge officious multilingual sign,
A gendarme holding its papers in its hand.
Yet there's a noticeable change. Of tone,
Of texture or feeling? One knows one has gone
As into a mirror that contains an ever so slightly
Distorted image,
Or perhaps from dreamt objectivity to the forthrightly
Seen – subjective, brilliant, undamaged.

The poem moves alone now, but without loneliness.
Self has been left among the objects that fashioned it.
Action and knowledge are one, free, far in the depths
     of consciousness.

     1 2 2

Plains of snow. The buntings whirl like rung
Cathedral bells in the stained-glass sunlight. Crows
Flop blackly with their black song
Away from the roadkills.
Barbed wire droops. In Asbestos a song is sung
On the juke box of old men dead and of the young
Who cough and sigh: "Help us get out
Of here. We die and nobody
Cares. Nobody even knows." In Drummondville:
"You Anglais, eh? Alors
Par' la joual ici maint'non, o.k.? C'la
Ou rien, *rrriennnn!*" At Trois Rivières
The thin iron bridge crossing the St. Lawrence,

Another lordly river, clogged now, great tiers
Of rhomboidal ice-blocks thrown up on the banks,

1 2 3

And in the town, in neon-blaring twilight,
The disco already throbs. Northward the poem
Moves, faster now, a flight
Unaware of time
In the flow of creation, short day and long night
Mingling, past *la cité*, into the hills bright
With the instincts of the glorious wolves,
Dark with the forest's deepness, all selves
Of history risen now in one true person, past
The great white silent *lac*
Where stars fade in the aurora, and at last
Out onto the open north, ecstatic,
Beyond earth and history, the nets of essence,
Free, alone with every thing, the aurora flashing,
Trumpets, the beat of the universe, immense, immense,

1 2 4

And there in the sky is the known face half-hidden
In rippling lights, askance, the eternal other
Toward whom the poem yearns, maiden
Of the water-lights, brother
Of the snow-fields, Androgyne! the forbidden
Ancient of ancients granting that the poem gladden
In its free consciousness which burns
With the whole selflessness of loving, its forms
Risen profoundly from remembered voices, its tones
Heard from the great silences,
While the aurora ripples and flashes, while the snow
Gleams with its own reflected innerness
Of brilliance, brilliance, to the horizon, far
Beyond the final extremities of distance
In the beating universe,
                              the poem alone and free . . .

Princess, the poem is born and you have woken,
A world's undone.
                        And it is no easy thing,
With brave romance and conquest broken,
Still to love and sing;
The tapestry is unthreaded, lovesong's unspoken
Horror spills out.
                        Yet you in yourself betoken
Love's amending, for you are Rose Marie,
Pure in transcendent being, free
From history, though the Dornröschen is keeping
Your beauty for us forever.
                        The sun
Will rise on the snowy firs and set on the sleeping
Lavender mountain as always, and no one
Will possess or command or defile you where you belong,
Here in the authentic world.
                        The work is done.
My name is Hayden and I have made this song.

MOTHER

O thou great Nothing, thou Indifference,
thou Forgetfulness, has not she in her own nature the right
to be meaningless? To be what in their nature words
cannot contain, the less than meaningless?
— SADHU JINRI-GHORAMNYA

(Margery Carruth, 1896–1981)

1. THE EVENT

Mother, now at last I must speak to you. The hour, so late but even so, has come.
Mother, after sixty-one and a half years of my life,
After one and one-quarter years of your death,
After your incomprehensible durance and anguish, which deranges me still,
After the wordless years between us, our unutterable, constricted, strangling
    chaos,
After the long years of my private wrecked language, when my mind shook in the
    tempests of fear,
After everything between us is done and never to be undone, so that no speech
    matters,
Nevertheless I must speak.

The sea is not here, nor has it ever in my life been where I was,
Nor was it more than briefly ever in yours (you, bound inland, away from your
    desire),
Yet how you spoke, sixty percent aphasic as you were,
Of "the water" and "the ship," and of "the glittering water" or "the golden
    shining water"
Between the ship and the pier when you looked down from the fantail,
(Was she the *Vulcania?* I almost seem to remember),
How you spoke in the phantasmic childhood you were living again
Of the water gleaming, of your mother, of her leaping down into that golden alley
    of death,
(But she did not; she leapt from the sixteenth floor of a hotel on Broadway),
How your pallid, brown-spotted, wrinkled, half-paralyzed countenance grimaced,
So that I could not tell whether you were smiling or struck with terror,
Until I recognized that it was the ultimate human expression, the two masks
    superimposed,
Mother, how you spoke then, giggling and whimpering, your voice skipping from
    node to node of your mind's dispersion,
How you mingled the water, the glimmering, the exhilaration of a voyage
    beginning, the horror of a voyage ending,
(Your mother, my Nana, the strange woman of glistening auburn hair),
How you spoke gave me to understand the as it seemed inhuman human lucency
Of your half-dead mind,

And the way, intermingling there, these visions of childhood, death, mother,
     and water
Were the wisdom beyond speech,
Were knowledge in its clearest configuration,
Which did not for one minutest part of an instant relieve your agony.
"O Hayden, take me home," you wailed, singing it out fully and tremulously.
But you thought home was England.

Was your damaged brain the same as a damaged soul?
I ask myself, and have asked in long, long sequences of perturbation and doubt,
(I who have called and called to my own soul and never heard an answer),
You lay there three years, twisted,
Until your body became so rigid that no man could have been strong enough
To undo the knot, as no person, man or woman or even child,
Could penetrate your mind in its writhing, convulsive indagation.
Oh, the suffering! You in the focus of the pain of all our lives,
You on the threshold, knowing it clearly, peering into the darkness,
But so ravaged in the coils of thought that no current could be induced,
And thus you lay there smashed, a machine of random parts, of no definable
     function,
Unable to generate so much as the least beginning spark of an idea,
Unable to conceive any *suppositum* of your predicament,
And fear wailed out of you, unintelligible sentences that vanished in rising
     tremolo,
As if you were an animal somehow granted the power to know but not to think,
Or as if you were a philosopher suddenly deprived of every faculty except
Original fear and pathos. I cannot surmise a state of being more inconsonant
With human consciousness.
Oh, many as evil, many and many, God knows, but none essentially worse.

To which was added, of course, humiliation.
"I am not nice," you repeated in your weeping quaver. "I am not nice,"
Covered from head to foot with your own shit.

Once when I came you would not acknowledge me. Not even a flicker of your
     eyelid.
I thought you were dead.
I shook you as it seemed unmercifully and shouted next to your ear. I shouted.

At last, unmoving, you said in a quiet, perfectly normal voice, as in old times,
    "I hear you."
Nothing more. After an hour I left.
Never have I heard anything more terrible than that "I hear you."

Three years. For you they could have been three million. You lived only
In the present moment,
The moment before death.
And the doctors who had "saved your life" would give you nothing.
Three million moments before death.
Should I have smuggled in marijuana for you? Heroin? I think I should.
A century ago the doctors would have fed you laudanum like sugar cubes,
Assuming you had lived through your first stroke. But you would not have.
You would have died quickly, appropriately, humanly.
For every technological advance, intelligence makes a moral regression.

Three million moments. Three million deaths. O my mother.
You lying there in a twisted, useless body.
You on the shore of death, perpetually.
You in the shadowy tumult of memories.
You in your language broken, stammering, whole aggregates of once-luminous
    words blown out.
You nearly blind, your son's face unrecognizable.
You with your hearing still acute, able to distinguish voices.
You with your radio that the nurses always turned to a rock station, in spite of your
    frowning.
You unable to cover yourself, your withered cunt showing.
You wailing and wailing, no, not like a child, but in a voice torn and wasted, a cruel
    parody of a child.
You with your teeth broken and rotted like barely discernible, almost effaced lines
    of an ancient wooden sculpture (and the doctors would permit no dentistry
    for fear the shock would "kill" you).
You there, always and forever there, in the termination that obliterates everything
    else.
O my mother.

2. THE WATER

I think I know why in death's unrelenting moment you thought of the water,
    the ship, and your mother,
And of your mother's death,
("I think," so common, so perilous a verbal alibi),
For this is the technology of intellection in our time, state-of-the-art,
How are implanted in every childhood the great emblems of our being, one way
    or another,
Then to roil fomenting like magma in our deepest centers, managing us whether
    we will or no,
For did not the land rise from the sea? Oh, consider that spasm:
Did not you erupt from the amniotic fluid of your mother's uterus, as I from yours?
That sea whose currents, swaying, are the flow of motherhood through all our idea
    of time,
From the earliest parturition,
From the first warming of blood,
From the primeval rising and falling, the moist vapors and condensations,
The warmth of the remote sun nevertheless occurring here on this stony shore,
    this wall, this hospital,
And our returning through all existence to the tidal source, death in the water
    and forgetting.

Once I sat on a bluff by the Susquehanna, that broad green fluvium,
I looked backward beyond the near diagonal slope to the broad field undulating,
A farmer ploughing there, guiding the share in the furrows behind his horse in
    the old way,
Patiently, steadily, a man familiar with the good way of loving,
And the field was writhing in her corresponsiveness,
But as if all the declensions of intelligence with its smeared graphia had blurred
    my vision,
I could not see if she moved in pleasure or pain,
O rainlike sun, O earthen sea.

How was it when you were ploughed?
Not aphasia can be the cause why you never said
In all the clinging cries of your long death
The word for your husband.

O my mother, how we have in paltry intelligence made a foul language,
For do not we say "conceiving"
To mean both the transactions of love in nature and the negotiations of thought
      in emptiness?

The land risen, streaming in all her vulval channels, the fecund mud,
The loam ploughed and harrowed (oh language of violence) and dark and clean,
The corn sprouting, green leaflets, rows curving with the contours of earth's body,
The worms working the soil and the swaggering crow lording and eating,
Could you in the chaos of misery, the wound of your ancient sex aroused and
      stinging under death's touch,
Make any conceiving of these conflicting emblems?
Or shall I say that before intelligence, pleasure and pain simply were, and were
      one,
The undifferentiated sensing, without discrimination?
No. But for you were we all hagseed.
But for you.

When an old woman, staring blind, her skeleton, the skull and bones, showing
      almost white
Beneath the mantle of her dissolving skin,
Dies at last,
We rejoice and say that she is a bride again, and we give her flowers,
Virgin of the sea, girl of the sun,
– And mother, I could bide no more in these damnable
Inconsistencies, fear-wrought, flimsy, hysterical,
And I saw we are right to rejoice, a small, reluctant celebration of the drowned
      mind,
For the passage out of consciousness is at least in itself a minor advantage,
Though it is not a passage out of existence.
Ah, that it were, my mother,
Then would we have true marriages!
Rejoicing points our way through the little door at the back of the garden,
Hidden in the vine-leaves that we in all our power of thought are afraid to part.
To rejoice for death is to mourn existence,
As we do in the vine-covered depths of imagination,
All secretly, all in vestigial instinct unknown to us, as animals who regard the
      world with scorn,

Look at them, great panthers, wolves, study those eyes, they hold our own
      ancestral, proud resentment,
Existence is the crime against the existing, and no matter who is the criminal,
(The death of God, like the death of Hitler, is an affair of no consequence),
This thisness that is, all this something that could just as well be nothing,
The seed or the sequoia, the neutron or the galaxy,
What is and is and is and is and is,
Oh, in my rage at No One to address, I cry out: Intelligence,
(For mind is implicit in it all),
Give over, it is enough, let existence subside,
All this that words point to meaninglessly like vanes jerked in the wind,
Sea, land, sun, consciousness, the universe, most meaningless word of all (the
      fantastical converting into one),
I cry out for us all, Desist, give again the void, the one word that means everything.

3. The Ship

Margery Tracy Barrow Dibb Thummell Sterling Carruth, you used to rattle out
Your name like a litany, your Latin that nevertheless remained for you a little
      charm,
You linked, you connected, a place for you in the generations of Old England,
Yet you told me nothing of your family, you ran away from home when you were
      sixteen,
A lost child whose kinship was the waifs, those Dickensian forlorn whom everyone
      must love,
And only later did I learn that Tracy was the knight (the punk) who inserted the
      stiletto (the shiv) into Thomas à Becket,
Or that Barrow was rector of Christ Church, tutor to Isaac Newton, artificer of
      much of the *Principia,*
(When first I read what John Aubrey wrote of him, I was as if swept gently into an
      eddy of time by my admiration),
You in the long moment of death remembering your voyage (were they two?
      I think so) to England,
(And now my memory comes clearer, your vessel was the *Mauretania*),
How you crossed the shining water from earth to the great ship,
And went forth on the dark sea,
A child you were,
Then an old woman dying,
An event, an instant.

Clearly the first sailors were the dead. Why do I find here no scholars?
(Intelligence a structure of optimism, the human error, and thus ships *must* have
      carried corporate earnings to Thebes.)
The dead was placed on a dead tree at the riverside and sent on its voyage to
      the sea,
The temple of Osiris was built with a moated pool in the forecourt, on which
      voyaged a toy boat, the Ship of the Dead, wafted
This way and that by the currents of air that were Ra's whisperings,
And it is told that such a temple existed in Taunton, Massachusetts, which I
      believe,
For surely I am an Heliopolitan and Isis is my mother, and I dwell in the curse of
      Thoth forever,
(And yet, You Jackal, Eater of Carrion, if words were inevitable in your numen,
      how more wondrously than the hieroglyphikos, the priest-writing?),
And all oceans run westward in our minds,
And if rivers appear not to, still we must cross them,
The ferry, shadow of the sun's barque, each sundown into the dying aureole,
A lingering, languishing disappearance (appearance in Dis).

I have seen the jet at 35,000 feet, a spark in the sunset, under Hesperus,
      infinitesimal,
And then no more,
The empty acorn cupule, vacancy so vast, turning in the rivulet. (Akran, Goth.,
      fruit.)

Has anyone ever set foot aboard without a dark inarticulate knowledge of the true
      cargo?
The little last-minute hesitancy of embarkation.

Mother, I stood on the pier with you, in the turbulence of whirling images,
I leaned down to you, down to your words muffled by the wind,
I watched you cross, I waved to you, I smiled and took off my hat,
Little blonde girl frowning at the rail, your muff and shining black shoes,
The flowers crushed to your chest.

4. THE PHANTASMAGORIA
She shook him and the boy tumbled down the stairs, bouncing oddly from side to
      side. A box containing a loose weight.

At Hartford on the deck of the packet, awaiting departure, they sat under an
awning and stared at the rainbow, one of which was located in the river
halfway to the opposite shore.

The young woman, dressed in a long dark flannel skirt and a blouse buttoned at
the throat with a wide white collar, held the reins with both hands, but
lightly, as the carriage lurched up Hardscrabble Hill.

The dresser was painted, medium gray enamel, a white cloth with cross-stitched
hem in blue thread, a large mirror behind, speckled in one corner where the
silver had flaked. A hairbrush, comb, and handmirror of tarnished silver.
In the middle of the cloth lay her favorite pendant, a blue moonstone very
delicately carved to reveal the face within. Decades later it was presented to
a granddaughter and now lies at the bottom of the Gulf of California off Isla
San Marcos.

In the spring of 1926 she ran across a lawn, into an orchard, where apple petals fell
thickly about her. She wore a short skirt, tennis shoes, a sweater, a double
strand of amber beads. In the brightness her legs flashed whitely.

Her diary. Small black-covered record books, scores of them over the decades. She
wrote at a carved oval table in the corner of the dining room, next to a fern
and a telephone. For fifty years she used a green Parker pen with a gold loop
in the cap for suspending it on a ribbon, though she never carried it that way.

When her first great-grandchild was born in 1970, she tried to feel glad, but it was
useless. She bitched and nagged as usual. No room for great-grandchildren
in her vision of the House of Reality.

At age four she stood on a piano stool in a white ruffled dress and played a half-
sized violin. The music was not preserved in the photograph. Later one of
her favorite recordings – she had many – was Menuhin's performance of
the concerto by Mendelssohn.

At seven she dined at Delmonico's and marveled at the ballet girls dancing
overhead, their skirts whirling in circles above the glass ceiling.

At thirty-three she went to bed for six months. "Pernicious anemia." It was
successful and from time to time thereafter she repeated it.

She and her two friends, Madge and Milicent, canned peaches all day, filling the
kitchen with steam. A cloying odor. This was in 1939.

In 1925 she refused to sleep any longer in the same bed with her husband. She kept
the white enameled, iron double bedstead for herself. In 1928 she began
refusing to accompany him on his Sunday afternoon walks.

When her husband died, week after week she wept for his loss while she watched
baseball on the TV. "He was a good man," someone said. "He was the only
person who could comfort me in my trials," she answered. It was true.

The assembly of skeletal crones in their wheelchairs near the nurses' station. The
    smell. The inosculation of thecal miseries. The wails and babblement. Death
    permeative. Dachau.

Her pride. Never to include the lack of money among her complaints. To keep her
    house orderly and clean; to cover up its shabbiness. In old age she implored
    and cajoled, that others might wash the windows.

Her fear of coal gas. How she ran to the cellar door to sniff. How she threw up the
    sashes when someone farted.

Over and over she read the novels of Arnold Bennett, H. G. Wells, Helen Hunt
    Jackson, H. Rider Haggard, W. Somerset Maugham, Hugh Walpole, etc.
    But when television came, she gave up reading.

In her first years of marriage she wrote stories for girls and sold them to a children's
    magazine. Then she lost interest. A few years later her husband gave up
    writing poetry, although he had enjoyed a modest success with light verse in
    the slicks.

When she was a girl she skated to school from 96th and Central Park West to
    (I believe) 83rd near Amsterdam. Sometimes, if the northeast wind were
    strong, she could coast the whole way.

She delighted in avocados exceedingly, and was put out with her family because
    no one would eat oysters. She regarded her marriage as a social, though
    perhaps not a cultural, catastrophe. She ate avocados standing at the
    kitchen cabinet and scraped the hulls with her spoon. She called them
    alligator pears.

Anemia. Miscarriage. Chronic psoriasis. Hemorrhoids. Gallstones. Chronic
    cystitis. Uterine cancer. Cataracts. Toothache. Many cerebral incidents.
    Rectal cancer. Two major strokes.

When was her finest hour? She does not know. She remembers only successive
    faint sensations of imprisonment and flight.

5. THE MOTHER

The Indo-European root *pha*, suggesting light and clarity, surfaces in *phenomenon*,
    the thing that appears,
And also in the Greek for "I say," *phemi*, thence in *phonation, verb, word*,
(And, I suspect, in *speech*, though my magic partridge is roosting in some other
    hemlock tonight),
For appearance is nothing until it has been spoken and written, nothing at all,
And now words are revenant, like the tides of shards drifting on the waste at Old
    Oraibe,

The issues my friends and I *settled* twenty years ago or thirty years ago
Are now impossible even to describe.

Nana, so remote, yet only second in the chain of motherhood,
(My own grandchildren sending crayoned flowers as I sent mine to you),
You brushed your waist-long auburn hair until it shone as if it were burnished,
      you wore dead foxes with bright little eyes,
You came with trunks and hatboxes and bright packages of toys, and you stayed
      two days, and you departed,
You vanished into the train, which went away calling Who? Whoooo?
And you carried a book called *Science and Health,* which you left open upon the bed
      when you flumped from the hotel window,
And beyond you is no name, no woman, no mother, far down the valley of dark
      wind,
None in the mountain pass, none on the sunlit plain,
Far and far to the grove by the sea where dwells the water-woman whose beauty
      is too great to be looked upon
And where the bronzen child calls always in the sea-wind Who? Whoooo?

And the words are tokens, and the tokens are despair,
And the silence which is beyond everything, the silence which is around
      everywhere, is unattainable,
No death can reach it.

Hypocritical reader, you think you know better than I, and you do,
But your knowledge is of *tones,* not meanings; it is soothings and alarms,
The unrolling and rolling up
Of contrivance unending, images, blandishments, the calculus of inexperience in
      a thingless world,
The flat screen;
And your knowledge is the massive dictatorship that runs this camp of ignorance
      where I find myself;
Oh, the loathing with which I look out upon you, my horror, my despair.

6. THE SON

I held out my fingers while you burnt them with matches, one after another,
I snuggled close to you in the deserted railway station in Southbury while whirling
      snow filled the night,

I was astonished when you shrieked because you imagined I would marry the
 woman next door,
I never told you, when you visited me every week during the year and a half of my
 commitment, how grateful I was that you brought no other gifts,
I swallowed when you forced the castor oil into my mouth for punishment,
I cooked dinner in the fear of mystery when you lay ill and called directions to me
 in your unrecognizable voice,
I ducked when you stroked the back of my head and told me I had the handsomest
 nape in the world,
I tried not to scream when you hit me with my father's strop,
I tried not to cry when you fed me junket and sweet custard with the half-sized
 silver spoon, those times when I had measles and rheumatic fever,
I ironed the pillow cases, towels, and handkerchiefs, you ironed the shirts and
 sheets,
I came to you in shame when I pissed in my pants at age twelve because I could
 hold it no longer,
I stared when you held the ether over my nose in a tea strainer so the doctor could
 cut out my tonsils on the dining table,
I wondered when you held my face with your palms and looked at me a long, long
 time until I cast down my eyes,
I was shocked when you laughed delightedly at the hot juice fountaining up from
 the cherry cobbler you had made and it spurted all over the linen,
I was sobered when you took me to school and explained everything to the teacher,
I never understood (how could I?) the hunger of your love, or why you called me
 selfish . . .

Often people ask me how you were as a mother, and I ask myself how I was
 as a son, but what shall I answer?
We were like no others.
I know this. Anything else is inconceivable. My mind will not think it.
But more I cannot say, for what created our difference is still unknown to me.

7. THE DEATH
On the sea of motherhood and death you voyaged, waif of eternity,
You were the pioneer whether you knew it or not,
You were the unwitting pioneer, and most of the time unwilling,
You who for seventy years despised your stepfather, I am certain (in the nature
 of things) with justice,

You who knowingly first met your father when you were thirty,

The seedy businessman from St. Louis, that droll city,

You whose husband, loving and incapable, the knight in podgy armor, the poet from the land of the Brownies,

Talking away your blues with the wisdom he gave instead of love and that he himself could never use,

(Oh, might I say, with the dicky bird, that things past redress are now with me past care!),

You, my mother, who taught me without words that no secret is better kept than the one everybody guesses,

I see you now in your eternal moment that has become mine,

You twisted, contorted, your agonized bones,

You whom I recognize forever, you in the double exposure,

You in the boat of your confinement lying,

Drifting on the sea as the currents and long winds take you,

Penitent for the crime committed against you, victim of your own innocence,

(Existence is the crime against the existing),

Drifting, drifting in the uncaused universe that has no right to be.

NOTES

THE ASYLUM

Sec. 5. "...the Great Man ..." William Jennings Bryan, who first
came to prominence as a champion of silver-backed currency against
the gold standard, i.e. against Eastern banking interests. He was
nominated for president three times on the Democratic ticket.
Sec. 8 is about Ezra Pound.

JOURNEY TO A KNOWN PLACE

According to many early and some later natural philosophers the
physical universe comprises four elements, earth, water, air, and fire;
that is, terra, aqua, aer, and ignis. These are arranged in a circle. Each
has two attributes: earth is cold and dry; water is cold and moist; air is
warm and moist; fire is warm and dry. Thus each element shares one
attribute with its neighbors on either side in the circle. From these
attributes derive the four humors, blood, phlegm, choler or yellow
bile, and melancholy or black bile, and to these are attached the four
tempers, sanguine, phlegmatic, choleric, and melancholic. For many
centuries the practice of medicine was based theoretically on
combinations of attributes and tempers. The elementary spirits or
unseen intelligences considered the "finest essence" of each element,
are the gnomes of earth, the nymphs or undines of water, the sylphs of
air, and the salamanders of fire.

NORTH WINTER

Afterword: What the Poet Had Written. Presumably he was thinking
of the arctic expedition of 1909, led by Commander Perry, who had
reserved for himself and his negro "servant," Matthew Henson, the
honor of the final dash to the pole.

MY FATHER'S FACE

Sec. 1. ". . . after one that he loved best. . . . " "Introduction" from *Songs of Innocence*.

Sec. 6. "Alyosha left his father's house. . . . " Dostoyevsky, *The Brothers Karamazov*, Bk. III, Ch. 10, first sentence.

Sec. 7. ". . . like Yggdrasill." In Norse mythology the great ash tree symbolizing the universe.

Sec. 11. ". . . buntings. . . . " The snow buntings which in winter come down from the far north to northern New England. Often they may be seen wheeling in flocks, like pigeons, over a snowy field.

MICHIGAN WATER: A FEW RIFFS BEFORE DAWN

The title refers to an old blues. "Mississippi water tastes like turpentine, Michigan water tastes like sherry wine."

Sec. 5. ". . . gorilla. . . . " A remarkably handsome animal, known as Bushman and loved by most Chicagoans of the late 40s and early 50s. After his premature death from inactivity his body was stuffed and placed in the lobby of the principal zoo building, where it may still be for all I know.

VERMONT

". . . Mansfield. . . . " The state's highest mountain, west of Stowe, clearly visible from Lake Champlain.

". . . Big Jay down to Pisgah. . . . " Jay Peak, located between the towns of Montgomery and Jay about five miles south of the Québec border; Mount Pisgah, also called Mount Snow, near West Dover, ten miles from Massachusetts.

". . . moved to Nevada. . . . " The town of Lamoille near Elko, Nevada, and also the nearby Lamoille Canyon in the Ruby Mountains were named by an emigrant from Lamoille County, Vermont.

". . . more a Warrenite. . . . " Josiah Warren (b. 1798) was an early American anarchist and cooperativist who in 1827 in Cincinnati established the first "Equity Store," in which goods were exchanged solely for labor and cost alone determined price. He communicated his ideas to Robert Owen in England, who developed them in labor exchanges there and was a founder of New Harmony, Indiana. Warren later established other "time stores," as they were called —

because one hour of labor was the basis of all exchange – in Ohio and Indiana, as well as Equity Village, an anarchist community in New York.

THE SLEEPING BEAUTY

Sec. 1. The epigraph from Goethe's poem "Vanitas! Vanitatum Vanitas!" is difficult to translate, owing to the multiplexity of meaning in the German *Sache*. One possible translation: "I have made my concern [interest, intention, awareness, or by extension personality, self] out of nothing." See also Max Stirner, *The Ego and Its Own*.

Sec. 3. Rose Marie Dorn was born in 1932 in Parchwitz, Silesia, a region then nominally German but ceded to Poland after World War II. Because their family name was Dorn, her parents named her intentionally after the story of *Dornröschen*, and from this the poem sprang. But nothing beyond this in the poem should be construed as a personal reference.

Sec. 12. The "coincidental voices" mentioned earlier are placed within quotation marks. They are invented; they were heard in the susurrus of history. One hopes that the general time, place, and predicament of each speaker will be evident in what she says.

Sec. 15. Readers should note that the fragments quoted from blues throughout were set down as remembered at the time of writing and are sometimes incorrect. The case for leaving them uncorrected has to do with the essential meaning and structure of the work.

Sec. 21. "Brother Estlin": e. e. cummings. Reference is to a review, "America's Younger Poets," *Perspectives USA*, no. 12 (Summer, 1955), p. 134. Cummings died in 1962.

Sec. 25. Until the advent of western science, many people in India believed that the male's reservoir of semen, located in the head, was limited absolutely, and that each discharge brought him nearer to impotence and death.

Sec. 27. *Per una selva oscura:* through a dark wood. From the opening of the *Divine Comedy*.

Sec. 28. *Perché mi scerpi.* Canto XIII, 35, the "Inferno." Translated in the opening sentence of the section, as from the Temple edition. No further specific reference to the substance of Dante's poem is intended.

Sec. 32. *Lo buon maestro.* Dante's tribute to Virgil, his guide through the first part of the *Divine Comedy*.

Sec. 38. "Garding": -*ing* was a common folk substitution for -*en* and -*ain* during the 18th century and later in both England and America. Thus "Capting" in *Tristram Shandy*. Still heard in the mountains of Vermont.

Sec. 52. "Young Woman's Blues," Bessie Smith and her Blue Boys (Joe Smith, Buster Bailey, Fletcher Henderson). Original issue: Columbia, 14179-D, 26 Oct. 1926.)

Sec. 59. *Zoön politikon:* the political animal. V. Aristotle.

Sec. 77. Sidney Catlett, Sidney de Paris, James P. Johnson. Others present, in addition to Ben Webster, were Vic Dickenson, Arthur Shirley, and John Simmons. Blue Note, no. 953, 4 March 1944.

Sec. 81. *Languedoc:* the name of the language, the people, and the country. Pronounced trisyllabically. V. "Lo Lenga d'òc," *Working Papers,* Athens, Ga., 1982.

Sec. 85. "L'amour 'provençal' n'a point disparu sans laisser des traces profondes dans tous les domaines pénétrés de sa doctrine. Il a créé la politesse occidentale, la galanterie masculine; il a suscité indirecte-ment la préciosité du xviie siècle.... Dans la mesure où il était chevaleresque, héroïque et maître de ses élans, il a inspiré le code galant de la noblesse française jusqu'au *Cid.* Dans la mesure où il était magique et mystique, il a créé l'amour-passion. Dans la mesure où il était aspiration à la Pureté, il a préparé la poésie italienne du xiiie siècle, et, par Dante et le 'Dolce stil nuovo,' il influence encore la poésie moderne. Dans la mesure enfin où *il est confiance en la Nature et en l'Homme,* il demeure le seul principe sur quoi puisse se fonder une *mystique positiviste* (Auguste Comte en a repris à peu près toutes les données) et une morale de coeur." *Les troubadours,* R. Nelli and R. Lavaud, cited in *Troubadours Aujourd'hui,* L. Cordes, Arles, 1975, pp. 19–20.

In other words everything detestable, dreary, dangerous: the modern world, outcome of *trobar* and *amor.* It is the most appalling paradox in history. Many similar statements of it have been made, of course, from De Rougemont's *Love in the Western World* onward.

The quotation in the final lines may be translated roughly: "Alas, god of love, who has given me so much joy, who has brought me so much grief from it." It is the conventional lament of the *trobadors,* but meaning almost infinitely more to us than it could have meant to them. In this case the line is from a *romanza* by Rambaud de Vaqueiràs (d. 1207).

Sec. 105. Bunny Berigan, Sidney Bechet, Pee Wee Russell, Coleman Hawkins, Vic Dickerson, Johnny Hodges, Mary Lou Williams, Billie Holiday.

Sec. 113. "A nest of flames": *sommeil dans un nid de flammes*. Rimbaud, "Nuit de l'Enfer," *Une Saison en Enfer*.

Sec. 118. The Opera in Derby Line, Vt., has now been restored.

MOTHER

Sec. 3. "Barrow." Sir Isaac Barrow (1630–1677). According to Aubrey, Barrow died in Istanbul while on a diplomatic mission. His last words were, "Mine eyes have seen the glories of this world."

Sec. 3. "Taunton, Massachusetts." See *Columbus BC*, Jonathan Steele.

Sec. 5. "... my magic partridge...." *Origins: A Short Etymological Dictionary of Modern English*, by Eric Partridge, 2nd ed., New York, 1959.